Savannah Monitors

Mark K. Bayless

Savannah Monitors

Project Team
Editor: Thomas Mazorlig
Copy Editor: Mary Grangeia
Cover Design: Mary Ann Kahn
Interior Design: Mary Ann Kahn

T.F.H. Publications
President/CEO: Glen S. Axelrod
Executive Vice President: Mark E. Johnson
Publisher: Christopher T. Reggio
Production Manager: Kathy Bontz

T.F.H. Publications, Inc.
One TFH Plaza
Third and Union Avenues
Neptune City, NJ 07753

Printed and bound in China,
06 07 08 09 10 1 3 5 7 9 8 6 4 2

Library of Congress Cataloging-in-Publication Data
Bayless, Mark K.
Savannah monitors : a complete guide to Varanus exanthematicus / Mark K. Bayless.
p. cm.
Includes bibliographical references (p. 115) and index.
ISBN 0-7938-2886-4 (alk. paper)
1. Savannah monitors as pets. I. Title.
SF459.L5B39 2006
2005035529

The Leader In Responsible Animal Care For Over 50 Years!™
www.tfhpublications.com

Table of Contents

When I was a little kid, my favorite animals were dinosaurs–the "terrible lizards." I read all about them, especially in books written by naturalist-explorer Roy Chapman Andrews (1884–1960). Most kids, and many adults, too, just love these tremendous big reptiles of another time. They are seen everywhere today, in every museum and most classrooms throughout the world. They both frighten and delight the imagination of people of all ages. They were one of the most successful forms of life seen on planet Earth since its origin.

According to current theories, about 65 million years ago, a cataclysmic event occurred. An enormous asteroid collided with planet Earth near present day Yucatan, Mexico. This asteroid killed over half of all life on the planet, including the dinosaurs, in what was likely only a matter of months. What began as an asteroid impact altered life on Earth forever.

The dinosaurs were gone, but there were survivors of this cataclysmic event: bacteria, some invertebrates, some fishes, some amphibians, some plants, some reptiles, some diminutive mammals, and early birds. These groups continued with their primary directives: to eat, grow, reproduce, and prosper. The world had changed, and with it, new forms of life evolved and developed. The mighty "terrible lizards" are gone, but not forgotten. The most

Introduction

dinosaur-like reptiles we see today are monitor lizards, members of a family of lizards called Varanidae (and monitors are sometimes called varanids).

Monitor lizards survived this cataclysmic extinction event 65 million years ago, although their marine-counterparts, the mosasaurs, did not. These early monitor lizards lived among both the diminutive mammals and towering dinosaurian relatives in what is now the Mongolian Gobi Desert. Later (fossil) monitor lizards would live in North America (genus *Saniwa*) and Europe (genus *Paleosaniwa*), with more recent forms living in Asia Minor (*Varanus griseus caspius*), Australia (*Varanus prisca*), and Africa (*Varanus rusingensis*).

Many people—perhaps yourself included—have decided to keep these little dinosaurs in their homes. As long as the hobby of keeping reptiles as pets and display animals has existed, people have probably kept monitor lizards. This book is about one of the most commonly kept monitor lizards, the savannah monitor, and its close relatives, the white-throated monitor and the eyed monitor. Within these pages, you will find everything you need to know to successfully keep one these fascinating lizards as a pet. There is also information on breeding monitors—a feat still rare among reptile hobbyists. So, enjoy this book and enjoy your "terrible lizard."

Chapter 1

Natural History

While you may think of your savannah monitor as a pet, it is essentially a wild animal. Even if you buy a captive-bred baby, it is still only one or two generations removed from the wild. To better understand your monitor and its care, you will need to understand something of its habitat and behavior in the wild.

The savannah (or Bosc's) monitor is found in western Africa, in the area between the Sahara Desert to the north and the rainforests to the south.

Savannah, white-throated, and eyed monitors are found in Africa, mostly south of the Sahara Desert. Africa comprises approximately 11,685,000 square miles (18,727,936.1 sq km), as compared to the United States, which comprises 3,539,341 square miles (5,696,017.2 sq km). Africa averages 3,000 feet (5632.7 m) above sea level across most of its total area expanse, with lofty plateaus dramatically dropping to sea level. The terrain is varied and includes deserts, savannahs, rainforests, mountains, and swamps. Africa's largest geographical feature is the great Sahara Desert, encompassing a vast 3,500 miles (1066.8 m) east-to-west and 1,100 miles (1770.3 m) north-to-south of North Africa's terrain. In Africa's center lies the Congo Basin, a hot, humid place known for its vast Ituri Forest. The southern hemisphere of Africa is dominated by deserts, but these deserts are not as barren as the Sahara in the north.

Monitor lizards are adaptable animals and can live in urban environments as well as in deserts. However, savannah and white-throated monitors tend to avoid human habitations. All monitor lizard species today are considered threatened, with four of them endangered (Bengal monitor, yellow monitor, desert monitor, and komodo monitor) on C.I.T.E.S.

Distribution

Monitor lizards are known in every country and habitat on the African continent. There are at least six species of monitor in Africa. There are the three that this book discusses—the

Scientific Names

Each animal only has one scientific name, which is written in italics and often follows the common name. Biologists determine the scientific name of each animal based on which other animals it is related to. Each scientific name has two parts: The first part of the name is called the genus, while the second part is the species. This combination of genus and species is unique for each animal. Scientific names allow scientists all over the world to talk about each animal without worrying about similar animals being confused with the one they want to discuss.

A scientific name is often abbreviated after the first usage. The genus is abbreviated to the first letter. So, after introducing the savannah monitor as *Varanus exanthematicus,* it can be referred to as *V. exanthematicus.* If the author is talking about all the lizards in this genus, he or she can use Varanus without a species name attached. The scientific name of the white-throated monitor is *V. albigularis* and that of the eyed monitor is *V. ocellatus.*

Scientific names are used frequently in the herp and fish hobbies.

savannah (or Bosc's), eyed, and white-throated monitors—plus the wide-ranging Nile monitor (*Varanus niloticus*), the West African forest monitor (*V. ornatus*), and the North African desert monitor (*V. griseus*), which also ranges into Arabia and western Asia.

In 1981, I purchased an 8-inch (20.3 cm) savannahh monitor, sometimes called Bosc's monitor. The pet shop proprietor told me this lizard came from South America! I soon realized this was an error of 2,500 miles (4,023.4 km). While setting up an enclosure for this little animal, I decided to find out exactly where savannah monitors live in Africa. From 1982 to 2002, I found thousands of localities for African savannah monitor lizards (3,268 localities to be precise), and I published my findings in the *Journal of Biogeography*, so that anyone interested in this subject could review the information for themselves (Bayless, 2002).

So, where do African savannah monitors live today? The Bosc's monitor, *Varanus exanthematicus*, white-throated monitor, *Varanus albigularis*, and eyed monitor, *Varanus ocellatus*, live in deserts, savannahs, dry forests, and rainforests. They are found in some coastal areas, as well. There is some overlap in East Africa where the three savannah monitors dwell; it is not clear if they, in fact, encounter one another or not.

The savannah monitor is still common throughout much of West Africa, with a

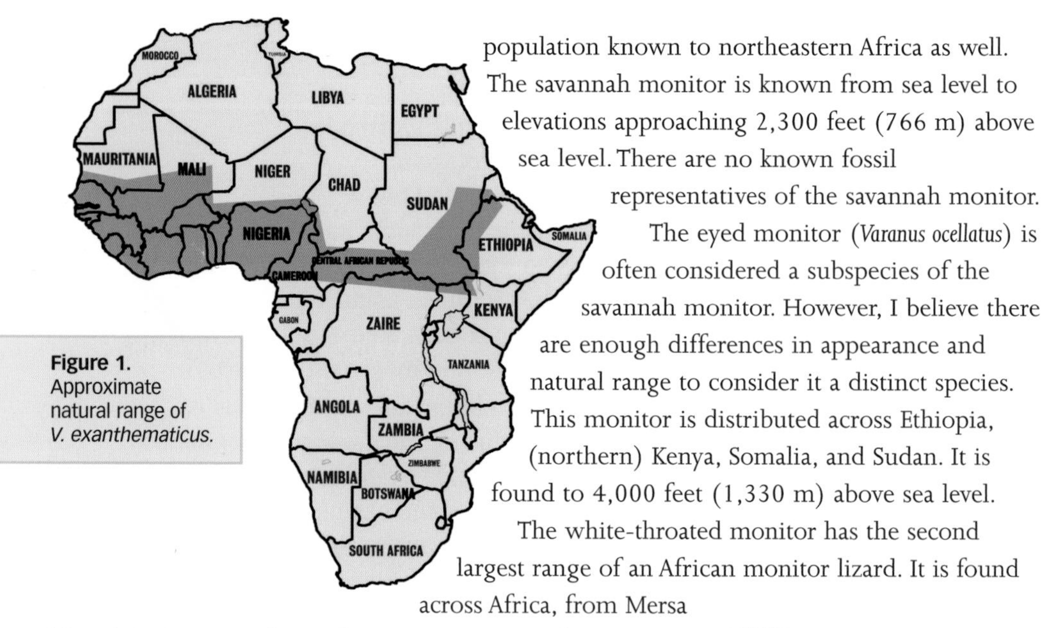

Figure 1. Approximate natural range of *V. exanthematicus.*

population known to northeastern Africa as well. The savannah monitor is known from sea level to elevations approaching 2,300 feet (766 m) above sea level. There are no known fossil representatives of the savannah monitor.

The eyed monitor (*Varanus ocellatus*) is often considered a subspecies of the savannah monitor. However, I believe there are enough differences in appearance and natural range to consider it a distinct species. This monitor is distributed across Ethiopia, (northern) Kenya, Somalia, and Sudan. It is found to 4,000 feet (1,330 m) above sea level.

The white-throated monitor has the second largest range of an African monitor lizard. It is found across Africa, from Mersa Matruh in Egypt on the Mediterranean coast to the Cape of Good Hope at the bottom of the African continent in South Africa. Unlike the Nile monitor (*Varanus niloticus*), which requires sufficient water resources, the white-throated monitor is known to occur far from water. It is known from sea level to elevations approaching 3,900 feet (1,300 meters) above sea level. There is a single possible fossil record from South Africa for the white-throated monitor reported in 1981.

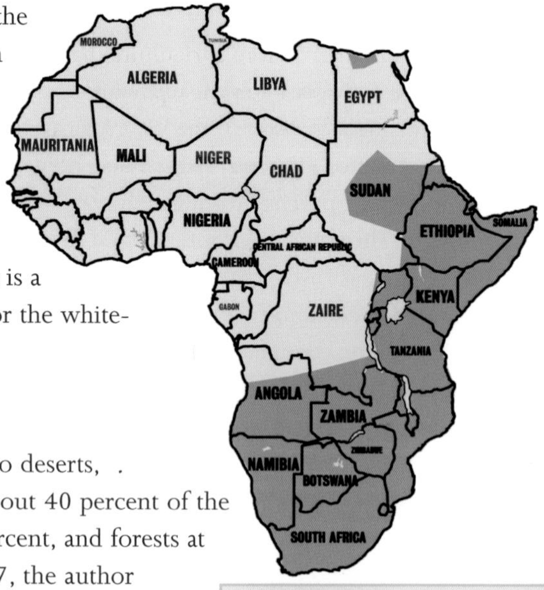

Figure 2. Approximate natural range of *V. albigularis.*

Habitat

The African land mass is divided roughly into deserts, grasslands, and forests, with deserts covering about 40 percent of the total area, savannah grasslands at roughly 40 percent, and forests at about 20 percent of the remaining area. In 1997, the author examined the habitats of African monitor lizards and found some information on the exact habitats of monitors, and with

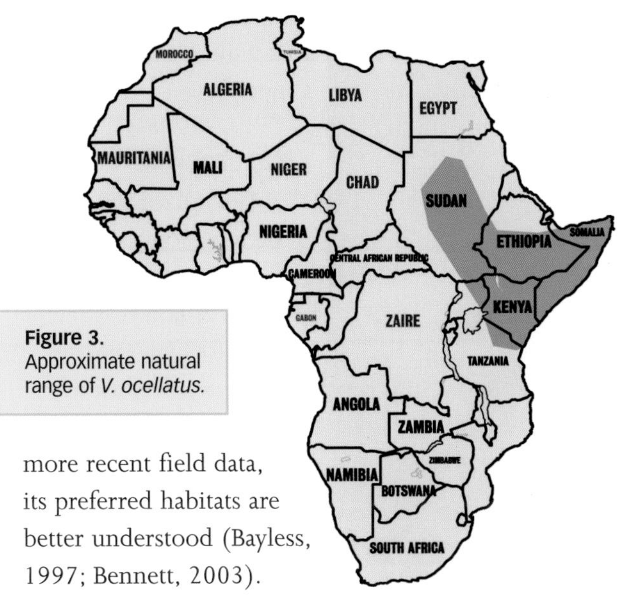

Figure 3. Approximate natural range of *V. ocellatus.*

more recent field data, its preferred habitats are better understood (Bayless, 1997; Bennett, 2003).

In West Africa, the savannah monitor prefers grassland and low-shrub savannahs. Savannah monitors frequent more agricultural habitats. In West Africa, fire is a common phenomenon, as the grasslands of this region burn annually. As a result, the soils become enriched with the ash of the burned plants. During the fire season (October to January), the best place to find a savannah monitor is underground, where they retreat so that fire cannot hurt them (Miles et al., 1978; Bennett, 2003; Miles, pers. obs.).

In East Africa, the white-throated monitor prefers savannahs, miombo forest habitats, and grassy shrubland, with deciduous shrubs interspersed with trees and dolerite *kopje's* ("koppies," or rock outcrops). These lizards prefer crevices dotted with *Stamfrachte* bushes where spiny acacia trees abound, living between the large kopje's where tiger cats, leopards, antelopes, and snakes also dwell. It is in these tight confined places that white-throated monitors live, where there is shelter, safety, and food.

The eyed monitor is known to dwell in drier habitats in East Africa, where permanent water and plant life are scarce (contrary to the Yemen monitor (*V. yemenensis*) that lives in drier areas but preys on the more abundant wildlife near oases and springs). In captivity, the eyed monitor lizard seems to prefer more water than either of its counterparts, the Bosc's or

More Monitors

Taxonomic research keeps expanding our knowledge of the diversity of life. Research on monitor lizards has likewise revealed much more diversity than we previously suspected. In 1964, there were 26 known species of monitor lizard. To date, there are 73 species and/or subspecies of monitor lizard now recognized. There are several photographs on the Internet and in books written about monitor lizards that depict unknown species still waiting to be described.

its white-throated monitors.

Microhabitats

The microhabitat is where a monitor lizard spends most of its time—its home, where it basks, forages, explores, feeds, and sleeps. For a home, most savannah monitors reside in termite mounds, in underground burrows, in acacia and boabab trees, under rocks, and in crevices. These places provide shelter and safety from predators and the environment.

White-throated monitors can be found in some very arid habitats. This one was photographed in northern South Africa.

All monitor lizards prefer a home that is snug, where predators cannot gain access or pull them out. The ratel or honey badger (*Mellivora capensis*) will readily do this to white-throated monitors (Watt, 1999). These tight-wedged places, or hide spots, of security for your lizard can be easily duplicated in captivity by using cork bark, mason bricks, flagstone, terra-cotta shingles, even buckets or storage boxes with entrance holes cut in them.

Temperature

Like the ancient Egyptian people, monitor lizards love the sun; unlike ancient Egyptians, monitor lizards are cold-blooded animals that need the sun to control their physiology and metabolism. Reptiles cannot maintain a constant body temperature through metabolism like warm-blooded animals can.

What temperature is good for the African monitor lizard? Some keepers have told me they keep their African monitor enclosures at 140°-160°F (60°-71.1°C). Are such temperatures suitable for African monitor lizards? The hottest temperature on record for all of Africa occurred in Libya at El Azizia on September 13, 1922 when it reached 136°F (43.5 °C). However, this is an isolated event, for nowhere on the African continent does the temperature exceed 120°F (48.9°C) for any length of time. The desert monitor (*Varanus griseus*) species is known to Libya, and if it were exposed to a temperature of 136°F (57.8°C) for more than a few minutes, it would reach its critical thermal maximum (CTM) point, go into thermal shock, and die.

According to thermal experiments done by Dr. Claude Grenot in the Algerian Sahara Desert in 1968, the desert monitor (*Varanus griseus*) can tolerate a temperature of 107.6°F (42°C) for a maximum exposure time of 4 hours, provided it is sufficiently hydrated. If the monitor is exposed to 108.5°F (42.5°C) for 4.5 hours of direct heat it will die (Grenot, 1968). The desert monitor is more adapted to hot, dry temperatures than its sister species on Africa. It is *not* recommended that you apply such hot ambient temperatures to your monitor lizards for *any* length of time.

SVL

One measurement used often in herpetology is the snout-to-vent length, or SVL. This is the length of an animal measured from the tip of the nose across the belly to the cloaca, or vent. It excludes the tail. The reason the tail is excluded is that many lizards (and to a lesser extent, snakes and salamanders) lose their tails, so including the tail length often gives an inaccurate impression of the animal's true size and possibly age.

Different reptiles have different optimal activity temperatures, and consequently, CTM limits. The activity temperature is the lizard's body temperature during which active behavior, such as hunting, feeding, and fighting, are most often displayed. The basking temperature is often a higher temperature than the activity temperature; it takes the monitor lizard time for its body to attain optimal body temperature each morning, after which it can engage in behaviors associated with this activity temperature. Body and basking temperature depends on the size of the animal and the ambient temperature and humidity of its environment. A larger animal is going to take a longer time to heat up and reach its activity temperature than a smaller animal. Savannah monitors emerge from their wild burrows when the ground temperature reaches from 80.6° to 87.4°F (27°-30.8°C), from between 6:36 am to 10:00 am (Yeboah, 1993).

In his field commentary, Mr. N. Bayoff noted the monitor lizard had a higher body temperature than the surrounding ambient temperature. This is a common factor for obligate predators that require higher body temperatures than the surrounding ambient temperature so they may hunt efficiently and catch fast-moving prey.

Monitor lizards can maintain high body temperatures, as do mammals. They require higher body temperatures before and after feeding, when their metabolism must be increased to properly catch and digest prey. It is well known that monitor lizards eat more, grow faster, and become heavier when temperatures are higher. The threshold of thermal exposure for many monitor lizard species appears to be 104°F (40°C); higher temperatures can be tolerated for short durations (Grenot, 1968; Buffenstein, 1982; Ibrahim, 2000).

White-throated monitors and other monitors control their body temperatures by moving into and out of sunlight as they need to warm up or cool down.

What about animals that get too hot? They must cool off quickly, and the best way to do that is to entirely submerge themselves in water. In captivity, you often see younger animals submerged in the water for long periods of time—one must wonder if they are too hot.

White-throated monitors appear to be more cold-tolerant than other monitors that are able to tolerate temperatures below 60°F (15.6°C) with no discomfort or ill effects (Dieter, 1997; McDavid, R. Williams, pers. com.). However, an animal submerged in water too long can become chilled, and for a reptile, this is bad. Exposure to cool temperatures, say below 60°F (15.6°C), for long periods of time can result in their death.

Humidity

Relative humidity is the amount of water-content held within the air. If the humidity is 100 percent, then the air is saturated with water, and it is most likely raining. Consequently, if the humidity is low, the air is drier. Moisture holds heat, so humid air may be in effect warmer than dry air. For example, if the temperature is 87°F (30.6°C) and the humidity rises, the ambient temperature may rise to 93°F (33.9°C). Humidity levels depend on air temperature and dew point levels and vary with the seasonal rains and dry spells. Air temperature and humidity are different from ground temperature; ground temperature is the temperature of the ground surface, which is different from the air temperature approximately ten inches above.

When it is hot, the ground may often be hotter than the ambient air temperature. When it is too hot for a species, the animal may seek water, shade, go underground, or stay in the trees where temperatures are not as extreme as they are at ground level.

Most regions in Africa have two dry periods and two rainy seasons, so these African monitor lizards have adapted to this climate by living below or above the ground during these seasonal fluctuations when temperature and humidity levels are comfortable or hellish. Humidity is the critical factor in the CTM thermal limits for almost all reptiles (Warburg, 1965:573).

Keeping Temperatures

Ambient daytime temperatures can range from 85°-105°F (29.4°-40.6°C) with nighttime temperatures ranging from 75°-85°F (23.9°-29.4°C). Avoid temperature drops below 60°F (15.6°C) if you can. Although monitors can tolerate such low temperatures for short periods of time, prolonged exposure to lower temperatures (below 40°F/4.4°C) can be fatal for them. See Chapter 4 for more details.

Hibernation and Aestivation

Hibernation is a state of torpidity that enables an animal to endure winter temperatures. Both aquatic and terrestrial hibernators must withstand prolonged starvation as well. Aestivation is a similar concept to hibernation, but is carried out during hot and dry periods, usually in the summer. Savannah monitors hibernate and aestivate within any single year, once during the hot, arid summer (aestivation) and then during the winter months (hibernation).

What brings on this aestivation and hibernation in reptiles is not clear; perhaps it is the moisture content of their prey. When these animals are hibernating, desiccation or water loss may become critical, so in captivity it is essential that they always have water available to them during this time. This is why, when not hibernating or aestivating, they are gluttonous feeders. A white-throated monitor can gain 2.5 pounds of body weight in a single month! They must feed diligently to build up their reserves so they can use these fat reservoirs for nutrition when the climate is adverse and/or when their reproduction season is upon them. During aestivation and hibernation, males lose approximately 35 percent of total body mass; females lose up to 50 percent.

Body temperatures of hibernating African monitor lizards generally range from 60.8°-70°F

Sleepwalking

Captive savannah monitors have been observed "sleepwalking" during hibernation periods when temperatures are higher, but they return to their burrows by day's end (Nieves, pers. com.).

(15.8°- 22°C) from October to February (Phillips, 1995, 2004; Lemm, 1997, 1998). African monitor lizards have exhibited hibernation behavior in both wild and captive conditions.

Hibernation and aestivation cycles are associated with reproduction cycles and with the onset of the rains. These animals seem to know when the rains are approaching (Berry, 1989:11). Can they taste the moisture in the air? Sure they can.

During both the wet and dry season when they feed less frequently, white-throated monitors may lose 30-50 percent of their total body mass during this aestivation period (Alberts, 1994; Phillips, 1995, 2004; Lemm, 1996-1998; B. Pierson, R. Williams, pers. obs.).

Predators

In Africa, like other places around the world, the law of the jungle applies: "Eat or be eaten." All animals, no matter what their size, have predators and must be wary at all times, especially when seeking out food. They must avoid being food for other animals. Monitor lizards are no exception. Knowing what natural enemies the African monitor has can help you understand some of the reactions your lizards may display around your home.

Humans are no doubt the greatest threat to monitor lizards. These animals are utilized for their skins in the skin-trade market, hunted as bush meat, and captured for the pet trade (Irvine, 1960; Bennett, 1997, 2003). The white-throated monitor (*Varanus albigularis*) is used for bush meat. In Africa, monitor lizards are frequent sources of protein, often seen in markets wrapped in twine and still alive (Switak, pers. com.). Thousands of savannah monitor skins are exported for leather goods such as wallets and watch bands.

Up to half of the dietary intake of the martial eagle (*Polemaetus bellicosus*) is the white-throated monitor (*Varanus albigularis*) (Watt, 1999:65). This is, in part, why you can observe your monitor lizard watching airplanes and why it threat-displays so alarmingly when you reach into the enclosure from above with a open hand—it resembles bird talons.

In captivity, many herpetoculturalists often live with other animals, like cats and dogs. Cats (*Felis domesticus*) and dogs (*Canis domesticus*) are natural enemies of monitor lizards in the wild, and in captivity, the keeper should take care that interactions between the animals are limited. People who also keep snakes should be aware that, in nature, these animals are natural predators or prey of monitor lizards, and, whether in captivity or not, will behave accordingly.

In their native countries, African monitors are hunted for food and skins.

Taxonomy

Taxonomy is the study of how animals are related to one another at the genus, subgenus, and species levels. In Tables 1 and 2, you will see how the savannah monitors are related to one another based on the works of Dr. Robert F. Mertens (1942:351) and later authors (Bohme, 1997; Faust, 2001; Bayless and Sprackland, 2000a-b;

Are Monitor Lizards Venomous?

In 2005, Dr. Bryan G. Fry and colleagues discovered that monitor lizards have the anatomy and ability to produce venom. Previously, the only lizards believed to be venomous were the gila monster and the beaded lizard, members of the family Helodermatidae. Toxicological analysis of the venom components from varanids shows their venom has the ability to dramatically lower blood pressure and reduce blood clotting ability, which in turn are associated with rapid loss of consciousness and extensive bleeding from the prey.

So what does this mean for varanid keepers? The majority of monitor lizards feed on insects and small rodents, so the amount of venom they may produce to subdue such prey is small. If the keeper wears thick gloves when handling monitors, there should be no chance of envenomization from your varanid. For larger monitors, feed them using tongs and wear thick gloves, which should be proper protection of your hands from their teeth. There have been no reports of envenomization from monitor lizards, except with the desert monitor (*Varanus griseus*) of North Africa and Asia Minor. The three species of savannah monitors pose no poisoning threat to keepers. Appreciation is extended to Dr. Bryan G. Fry (et al.) for sharing information with the author on this account.

Table 1. Morphometrics of the African Monitor Lizards

Species	Midbody Scale Rows	Ventral Scale Rows (from collar to groin)
Bosc's monitor *(V. exanthematicus)*	75 – 100^*	59 – 75^*
White-throated monitor *(V. albigularis)*	37 – 167^*	85 – 110^*
Angolan Monitor *(V. a. angolensis)*	109 – 144**	74 – 98^*
Ocellated Monitor *(V. a. microstictus)*	122 – 152^*	88 – 94^*
Eyed Monitor *(V. ocellatus)*	90 – 100	68-72"
Ionides Monitor *(V. a. iondesi)*	129 – 150*	88 – 99*
Yemen Monitor *(V. yemenensis)*	134 – 160	
Nile Monitor *(V. niloticus)*	128 – 165^	75 – 94^
Forest Nile Monitor *(V. ornatus)*	146 – 175^	80 – 97^

Source Key: **"**: Franz Werner (1907) **^**: Robert F. Mertens (1942) ******: Gaston de Witte (1953) *****: Raymond F. Laurent (1964a-b) and Donald G. Broadley (pers. comm . .)

Pianka et al., 2004:91-156).

One confusing aspect of African monitor taxonomy has been the ongoing discussion of the eyed monitor (*V. ocellatus*) and whether it is a valid species. This debate has continued since its initial discovery in 1827. Many examples of *V. ocellatus* have been identified as either savannah monitors (*V. exanthematicus*) and/or the ocellated white-throated monitors (*Varanus albigularis microstictus*) in the past, only adding further confusion as to which species is actually which species. Some *V. ocellatus* have a prominently raised vertebral column, which is not seen in either the savannah or white-throated monitor. Both the savannah and the eyed monitor have been imported together within the same shipments from Cairo (Egypt) and from Togo and/or Ghana in West Africa, which could support the idea that both of these monitor lizards are the same species or are two separate species that cohabitate, adding further confusion as to which species is which.

As one can see in Table 1, many of the scale counts overlap, making it difficult to know which species is which. Sometimes pattern and color help to identify locality-specific animals; then, in conjunction with the information in Table 1, a "best guess" assessment can be made. Color variations of the three species are discussed later in this chapter.

The savannah (bottom) and white-throated (top) monitors were considered subspecies of the same species until fairly recently.

In 1905, Lorenz Muller (1868-1953) postulated the African "stumpy-snouted" monitors were all similar, if not in fact variants of the same African species. The three "stumpy-snouted" monitors included the Bosc's monitor (*V. exanthematicus*), the white-throated monitor (*V. albigularis*), and the eyed monitor (*Varanus ocellatus*). From 1827 to 2006, confusion about *V. ocellatus* has ensued.

In 1942, Dr. Robert Mertens, a noted expert on monitors, was not sure about *V. ocellatus.* He listed both *V. exanthematicus* and *V. ocellatus* as synonymous. However, there are clear differences in skull morphologies (Mertens, 1942b). Dr. Mertens (1942a-c) deemed these differences in skull morphology of "little importance" and placed the eyed monitor (*Varanus ocellatus*) in junior synonymy to the Bosc's monitor (*Varanus exanthematicus*). I recognize the eyed monitor (*V. ocellatus*) as a full species, based in part on these *little important* differences in skull morphology, habitat differences, and its dark uniform grey color—sometimes with light blue-colored ocelli (spots) on its back—and a keeled vertebral column. At first glance, this lizard does resemble a savannah monitor (*V. exanthematicus*), but it is not.

Studying Monitors

Herpetologists are zoologists who specialize in the study of reptiles and amphibians, which comprise approximately 7,500 species worldwide. To be a professional herpetologist, one generally earns a Masters or Ph.D., after an undergraduate major in biology, ecology, or something similar. After earning a degree, the herpetologist works for a private organization, corporation, or public institution (zoo, university, etc.) with interests in biology or environmental issues.

In 1998, Dr. Robert Sprackland and I were sitting in the California Academy of Sciences' Department of Herpetology library pondering the white-throated monitor group, its subspecies, and their overlapping scale counts (in Table 1), when I noted a relief map of Africa on the opposing wall. We both walked over to the map and examined it closely. Then we saw it!

Plateaus, mountains, valleys, and rivers divide Africa, traversing the continent like a jigsaw puzzle. Near the borders of northern Malawi and southwestern Tanzania, we saw a pass between the mountain ranges where populations of the white-throated monitor of the southern hemisphere and equatorial region could encounter one another. As the overlap of scale counts showed, this would also account for the animals at these locations having both high and low scale counts. Animals that live at lower altitudes tend to have lower scale counts than do animals at higher altitudes; animals living at higher altitudes have larger scales to properly thermoregulate (Soule, 1972). This solved the overlapping scale count issue and the geographic isolation of these subspecies seen in some regions but not in others. In some regions, white-throated monitors were isolated, hence they were morphologically similar in those regions—as observations had reported, and as their taxonomy had shown from 1802 to 1964!

Furthermore, the skull morphologies of similarly aged white-throated monitor (*Varanus albigularis*) lizards, especially in the dorsal frontal and parietal region (top of the head, middle to posterior part of the head) were virtually identical whether you looked at a specimen from Ethiopia, Tanzania, or the Republic of South Africa. So what did this mean? The skull morphologies did not change with respect to where the white-throated monitor (*Varanus albigularis*) was collected; only scale sizes, scale counts, pattern, and color did – and that means that all white-throated monitor lizards are essentially the same species, with

The number of spots and the background color of savannah monitors are variable and somewhat depend on the habitat.

geographic variations according to ecological isolation (Bayless and Sprackland, 2000a-b).

Whereas some believe the white-throat (*Varanus albigularis*) monitor group consists of a complex of subspecies, others believe it is a monotypic species with variation. My opinion is by no means the definitive one on this subject, but merely one based on osteological (Mertens, 1942a,c), geographical (Schmidt, 1919; Bayless, 2002), and habitat (Bayless, 1997; Bennett, 2003:12-14) similarities and differences. When more information is gained, the models presented here may change, but that is how science works. It is not exclusive to scientists or herpetologists; anyone concerned with such things can contribute anytime.

Appearance and Variations

Each of the species discussed in this book has a distinct appearance, although the differences may be hard to see, especially for the novice hobbyist. Additionally, each has a variable pattern ranging from rare albinos to melanistic (all black), as seen in the savannah and white-throated monitors.

Savannah Monitor

A savannah monitor is a dark brown to cream-colored monitor lizard, ranging in size from 2.5 to 4 feet (76-122 cm) in total length. It has round ocelli along its back, ranging from 5-7 scales in size. The neck scales (called *nuchals*) are larger than the head or dorsum (back) scales, being more round in shape and sometimes slightly raised. The forelegs of this species are enlarged and Popeye-like. They are adapted for digging burrows in hard soils. The tail is somewhat fat and squat compared to other monitor lizards, which have tails that are more slender and streamlined. The savannah monitor has pale banding from the tail base to the tail tip. It has a cream-colored belly. Some specimens have two pre-anal pores just

White-throated monitors from the northern parts of their natural range tend to have rows of spots running parallel to the spine.

anterior to their cloaca, while others do not.

The savannah monitor varies in color; certain patterns are specific to certain localities. In West Africa's Guinea-Bissau, it is reddish or pink in color (Laulhe, pers. comm.), and so is the soil there. Some also have red-colored eyes, which may be a further possible adaptation to the red soils of Guinea-Bissau.

In the western nations of Ghana and Togo, savannah monitors can be dark gray and banded. Also in Ghana and Togo is the very rare white albino savannah monitor, which has very few spots with no banding and red eyes. Albinism is probably a simple recessive trait in these lizards. Many savannah monitors have red eyes, and many do not as well. There is also a very dark gray color form with no spots, which resembles the northeastern African populations of eyed monitors.

White-Throated Monitor

The white-throated monitor is typically a dark-colored animal, ranging from light chocolate brown to black. It ranges in size from 4.5 feet to 6 feet (1.3-1.8 m) in total length. White-throated monitors from more northern regions have flecking, while more

The Rare Sienna Leguaan

There is a color and pattern type of white-throat that is exceedingly rare in the wild and seen only once in captivity: the sienna leguaan (leguaan is a dutch term for monitor lizard). The pattern type was first described by ethnologist Dr. S. Dornan in the 1920's, and he described the sienna leguaans as follows, "...of a pale raw sienna color, marked with brown lozenge-shaped patches. I have seen these lizards near the Shashi River; also another kind of a straw colour marked with rings of a darker hue round the tail." One sienna leguaan (*Varanus albigularis*) was imported from East Africa to the United States in 1993. Successful tegu breeders Ron and Stella St. Pierre of Florida took photographs of this animal before it was sold to a woman in Colorado. I saw the animal myself. It was last known to reside in Southern California.

equatorial specimens have very large paired yellow to white ocelli in two to four pairs along the vertebral column. In Namibia, the white-throated monitor in and around the Ethosha Pan may appear bleached out, with minute flecking. The neck scales are typically raised, shaped like little rows of limpets, conical in shape. The forelegs, like the savannah monitor, are enlarged for digging. Like the savannah monitor, its tail is thick but long; it is used as a defensive weapon. The white-throated monitor also has banding from the tail base to the tail tip. The belly color and pre-anal pores are as in the savannah monitor.

Eyed Monitor

The eyed monitor is dark gray to a lighter battleship gray, ranging in size from 2.5 to 3 feet (76-91.4 cm) in total length. Some eyed monitors have light blue, open-ringed ocelli along their back to their tail base. These marks are often barely discernible even on clean animals. Eyed monitors have no banding on the tail. The vertebral column is slightly elevated from the nape to the tail base. In most other ways, eyed monitors are very similar in appearance to Bosc's monitors. However, they have longer toes (perhaps because they climb more often) and a wider head.

The eyed monitor, as its name implies, has an ocellated pattern, with rings and spots resembling eyes; they are very similar to the Bosc's monitor (*Varanus exanthematicus*) and some specimens of the N.E. white-throated monitor (*Varanus albigularis*) in Sudan and Ethiopia. This

Chapter 2

Behavior

Behavior is defined as the actions an animal takes in response to information or stimuli gained from the natural environment. The stimulus can be an internal factor as well, such as hunger. All organisms interact with and respond to their environment, no matter how subtle that response may be—even plants interact, although more slowly and more simply than a monitor would.

Monitors are probably the most intelligent of the lizards, and they often have inquisitive personalities.

Monitor lizards are predominantly solitary in nature and should be housed separately for the majority of their time in captivity. This will alleviate such happenstances as combat, cannibalism, and unnecessary injuries that can occur with your animals. In the monitor's world, space is the key. Aside from proper diet, heat, and basic requirements for your monitor lizard(s), space, or the lack of it, can initiate and determine how your lizard reacts to his environment and you. It is important for any keeper to understand his or her lizard, and that includes recognizing some of its behaviors. This will help you, the keeper, understand your lizard and will enhance quality time for both of you.

Intelligence

Some people believe reptiles are stupid. Back in 1956, Pat Collins showed they were not. He conditioned komodo monitor lizards (*Varanus komodoensis*) to do circus tricks by teaching them to jump through flaming hoops for food, just like the tricks performed by lions and tigers and even bears at circuses. If you feed a white-throated monitor six mice everyday for several days, and then feed it four another day, it will expect two more mice (Krebs, 1991; Firth, 2003; Sweet and Pianka, 2004).

Monitors definitely have the ability to learn and remember. As a monitor patrols its home range, it learns the details of its terrain, trees, burrows, and the like. Monitors will remember the various conditions the keeper exposes them to. There are even several observations of

Behavioral Enrichment

In studying behavior, I often placed a brown paper bag containing a rodent into the monitor lizard enclosures and watched them solve the problem of how to get the "prize" inside. Some ripped the bag with their claws, some bit the bag where they thought the rodent was, and yet others would find the opening of the bag and, through intense tongue-flicking and visual investigations, get the bag open, lunging inside for their food. I did this numerous times, and many of the lizards learned how to get their prize.

Offering a monitor this kind of stimulation is good for them as it gives them something to do, which stimulates their mental processes and reduces boredom and stress. In zoos, creating these opportunities for an animal to interact with its environment is called behavioral enrichment. After creating some of these scenarios, you will see increased activity in your monitor lizard. In the middle of the night, throw some pinky mice or superworms into their enclosure. In the morning when they wake up, after their basking period, they may detect that food is in the enclosure and start foraging, which also increases mental stimulation, exercise, and reduces boredom and stress. This is simple to do and enhances their overall welfare.

behavior that could be interpreted as play (including a savannah monitor playing with a ball); play is normally associated only with mammals and birds. When interacting with your pet, remember that monitors are probably the most intelligent of lizards.

Thermoregulation

When your monitor awakens each morning from its hide spot, burrow, tree branch, or water bowl, it seeks out its basking site to properly thermoregulate and attain its preferred body temperatures. Once the lizard is warm enough, it will start to actively forage, explore its territory, and/or look for mates. If the lizard becomes too hot, it will move into the shade, retreat underground, or enter water. Some species, including white-throated monitors, will move into the trees to be cooled down by the breeze. Regulating temperatures through behavior is called *behavioral thermoregulation*. This is important for the pet keeper to understand, because you must provide your monitor with opportunities to thermoregulate in its enclosure.

Large monitors sometimes will prevent smaller ones from using a choice basking site.

Basking postures tell other monitors (conspecifics, if discussing individuals of the same species) their temperament via body language. In the wild, when a larger monitor lizard wishes to bask at the same site as that of a smaller monitor lizard, the smaller lizard quickly moves away. In captivity, this is often not a choice, so it is best to offer several basking sites, especially if you have more than one animal housed together (which is not recommended). In this way, the monitors may all be able to thermoregulate properly without aggression, hardship, and stress.

Swimming

The savannah monitor lizard is not an accomplished swimmer, as many other monitor lizards are, but it can swim. It inflates its lungs, and—placing its four legs to its sides—undulates its body using its tail for propulsion. Savannah monitors can be seen near pools, especially during the hot *harmattan* (dry wind) months in West Africa from December to March. Some savannah monitors seem to like water, while others do not.

Aggression and Combat

Aggression is a behavior associated with territory, self-space, food resources, and reproduction. Many predatory mammals use non-mortal (ritualized combat) or mortal (fight to the death) combat when resources are limited; monitor lizards use both non-mortal and mortal behaviors in the wild, and often more so in captivity.

In ritualized combat, biting is not usually observed; when it is, it is no longer ritualized combat, but rather combat (Horn et al., 1994). Combat is used when animals are fighting over food, home range, microhabitat, or when a female is nest guarding.

Captive monitor lizards often fight to the death, as the loser cannot flee into the forest or up a tree. The victor often kills, and sometimes devours the loser. Hence, grouping your lizards together can be unwise. Monitor lizards kill their conspecifics by crushing their heads with their formidable jaws.

Territorial disputes between juveniles, subadults, and adults can lead to murder and/or cannibalism of their respective cagemates. I came home from work one evening to find three hatchling savannah monitors lying in the terrarium—one lying contently, the second one beheaded, and the third one with its left foreleg missing. The content one had eaten it! This was a territorial dispute that went really bad, and it was totally unexpected as they were housed in an 80-gallon (302 l) wooden enclosure.

Sleep

Sleep is a physiological necessity for higher vertebrates. It is a true instinct in mammals, controlled by the hypothalamus, which is the brain center for instinctive behavior. Some fishes, amphibians, reptiles, and birds do rest and sleep (Karmanova, 1975). Your monitor lizard will sleep nearly half of the day, so you should have proper places for it to sleep.

Avoid waking a sleeping monitor, as it can startle the lizard and in response, it may attack you. Nobody likes to be startled from a deep sleep.

Are Monitor Lizards Social?

Are monitor lizards social? Opinions are divided. Animals that pair-bond are usually equally sized male and female partners, whereas sexually dimorphic animals, including humans and monitors,usually engage in mate competition, which both of these species exhibit. Although monitor lizards can learn and have been seen together in the wild (in captivity this is often unavoidable), does this imply sociality? Dr. K Falk believed white-throated monitors in Namibia lived together in pairs (Falk, 1921).

It is an interesting topic, and I raise it here for its provocative connotations—I do not believe all monitor lizards are social, but perhaps a few species may be socially inclined. Some may hunt together, as the Nile monitor (*Varanus niloticus*) does when hunting crocodile nests.

Opinions are divided on how social savannah and other African monitors are in nature.

Because one species may be socially inclined does not imply all of them are. Each species should be examined individually. Seeing two lizards next to one another does not imply they are social.

Five Senses

When one is familiar with an animal's five senses, one can observe it with greater insight and learn what is normal for it. If the keeper recognizes some of these cues, it will enhance and enable you to maintain your animals at optimal husbandry levels.

Vision

Reptiles, like most vertebrate animals, have eyes surrounded by bone, which is called the orbit. The monitor's eye is protected by a third eyelid, known as the nictitating membrane, which protects the eyes in situations such as fighting, adverse weather conditions, excavating debris from a burrow, etc.

Monitor lizards cannot move their eyes very much, so to compensate for this they move their head and/or body to see what is catching their eye. Lizards often gaze at objects with one eye by turning their heads at the object of interest; they rarely look directly at an object with both eyes. Because monitor lizards have limited eye movement within the socket, they sometimes adjust their vision by popping their eyes outward, which allows them increased acuity and increases their proptosis, or the degree of vision possible (Smythe, 1975).

African monitor lizards can discern even the slightest motion at near or far distances, i.e., a sparrow that is a foot away or an airliner flying 10,000 feet above—monitor lizards watch airplanes and anything else that flies or resembles a bird overhead. In South Africa, white-throated monitors notice people at a distance about 90 feet (30 meters) away.

Do monitor lizards see color? It's believed lizards see orange, yellow, green, and red, and interestingly enough, most of the brighter colored monitors sport these colors (Smythe, 1975). Given their nocturnal activities, monitors probably see at different wavelengths than people do, and they can see at night.

Your monitor lizard may "tripod," or stand on its hind legs using its tail for support to get a better view of its surroundings (Christian et al., 1994). Tripod behavior is most often seen in terrestrial monitor lizards, but all monitor lizards can do this. Most monitors tripod during their courtship and ritualized combat displays.

Hearing

Some authors claim that monitor lizards are deaf, but the anatomy of their inner ear suggests otherwise (Schmidt, 1964; Miller, 1966). One field account exemplifies the ability of the white-throated monitor to hear: "To test its hearing I emitted a series of low whistles, pausing between each. The monitor immediately reacted by looking in my direction, but although I was completely in the open it seemed unable to make out what I was and soon carried on with its meal" (Borland, 1968). I observed keeper J. Adragna whistle to a savannah monitor and his own water monitors (*Varanus salvator*), and they always looked in his direction.

Smell

Smell is the sense that detects airborne chemicals. Odors are just chemicals. All forms of life use chemical stimuli as a form of communication, most often in the form of pheromones. Chemical signals are important for lizards, as many of their responses seem to be controlled by this stimulus. Scent is used extensively in locating prey and mates, while visual inspection alone seldom seems effective.

Note the ear opening on this savannah monitor. Most monitors seem to have decent hearing.

When you have just cleaned your lizard's terrarium, you place it back into its enclosure, and what does it do? It defecates! This is often followed by the scent mark—they wipe or drag their cloaca along the ground to establish this clean territory as their own. During the mating season, scent marking sites tell other monitor lizards they are there without the need for visual stimuli (Schwenk, 1995; Young, 1997). The pheromone scent of white-throated monitors is said to resemble sweet syrup (Moser, pers. obs.). I think it smells more like roasted almonds; so when your lizards are

Reptilian Bears

Some people have compared the monitor lizard to a fox, a lion, wild painted dogs, or crocodiles. I equate African monitor lizards with bears for many reasons:

- **They sometimes hunt in groups.**
- **They compete for mates.**
- **They are apex predators.**
- **They establish a hierarchy.**
- **They play.**
- **They engage in ritualized and/or mortal combat tactics.**
- **They scent mark territories by pheromone and tree scratching to establish territories.**
- **Bears have all these qualities, as well.**

sexually responsive, your home may smell like a pancake house!

Taste

The monitor tongue is bifurcated, or forked. The tongue aids the monitor in locating prey, swallowing food, and finding mates for reproduction. The tongue is approximately three times the length of the head and is an appendage of amazing dexterity. Monitor lizards actively use their tongues to push food to the rear of the mouth for ingestion.

The forked tongue enables the monitor to have stereoscopic taste—to sense an odor by tasting it. The forks of the tongue serve to help it distinguish if the scent is to the left, right, or straight ahead. Once the prey is within visual sight, the eyes take over in locating the food source or locating males/females for reproduction.

In captivity, unfamiliar foods were eaten only after touched by the tongue; however, starving animals will devour anything remotely edible without tongue flicking (Schwenk, 1995; Cooper, 2001). Most monitors do not appear to have taste buds, but they seem to enjoy certain foods more than others (Schwenk, 1985; Young, 1987). Instead of taste buds monitors have an organ in the roof of the mouth called the Jacobson's organ. When the monitor pulls its tongue back into its mouth, it pushes the tongue tips into the pouch-like Jacobson's organ. The lining of this organ is able to detect chemical signals, much like a combination of the nose and tongue of mammals.

Whether they can taste or not, they use their tongues to determine if an item is prey or not, whether another monitor is ready for mating or not, and to gain further information about their environment.

Touch

Monitor lizards have a highly developed nervous system. They have a keen perception of touch and vibration (Wolters, 1990). A monitor lizard can sense the touch of an object on any part of its body, such as when a tick crawls across its feet or legs. Ticks often move across a monitor during the night when it is asleep and less likely to engage in grooming behavior.

The tongues of monitor lizards, like the tongues of snakes, are forked and used to detect scents in the air and on surfaces.

Defensive Behaviors

Monitor lizards are highly intelligent and adaptive animals. They must contend with an array of animals of all types on the ground and in trees and the air. Most often, they initiate defensive behaviors when they are unable to flee from a perceived threat, or in captivity, when they are constrained to a given space, such as a terrarium.

In captivity, a keeper will witness the monitor lizard's defensive behaviors. An animal has few choices in an enclosure, so when a keeper or a perceived threat approaches, it reacts accordingly. After your monitor has settled in, it accepts its new surroundings as its new territory, and will defend it from others if necessary. If a monitor perceives you as a threat, it will defend itself.

With time, the keeper will come to recognize these protective postures and learn to avoid them, which also reduces the overall stress on both the monitor lizard and the keeper. The most frequently encountered defensive behaviors a keeper is likely to witness are the hiss, tail whip, and bite, but there are other behaviors these animals have in their arsenals to thwart their enemies that you should be aware of. Once your monitor becomes used to your presence, these behaviors will be seen with less frequency.

Threat Display

Monitor lizards express their feelings and status mostly by using body language. If a monitor is approached suddenly and/or by an unrecognized person, it will initiate the threat display. It may also do this if it just wants to be left alone.

The threat display is an impressive posturing behavior used by the monitor to make itself appear more intimidating, dangerous, and fierce. With a rapid inhalation of air through the mouth and inflation of the throat, it arches its neck and body, moving the body and tail into a laterally flattened pose. This makes the monitor look much bigger. Then, a hissing sound is exhaled through the nasal passages and mouth—sometimes monitors even blow bubbles out of their mouths.

Savannah monitors will puff up their bodies and gape when they feel threatened.

In the wild, a monitor could run up a tree, down a burrow, or into a cranny of rocks. In captivity, it is kept essentially in a box and has nowhere to go, so when it is confronted with a perceived threat, it must initiate its threat display. A display and hiss from a 6-foot (1.8 m) long white-throated monitor is an impressive sight to see and hear—and one any keeper should heed.

Tail-Whipping

All monitor lizards can tail-whip. Some exhibit this behavior more than others. With the savannah and white-throated monitors, the tail is their most frequently used defensive weapon. It can be an amazing instrument (of pain) when a keeper allows the monitor to use it properly. The tail ridge is lined with a double row of triangular scales or keel. The tail-whip can cause nasty welts, lacerations, and—with large species such as the Komodo monitor (*Varanus komodoensis*) or the water monitor (*Varanus salvator*)—even broken bones.

Most often, monitor lizards swing their tails at the eyes of their perceived threats. This will hurt and may cause momentary blindness. Following the tail whipping, which can occur as many times as the monitor perceives as necessary, the animal will attempt to seek refuge from its nemesis.

Monitor lizards cannot regenerate their tails as other lizards can; so when you see a monitor lizard with half a tail, it might have lost it defending itself against a predator.

Biting

If the hiss and tail-whip defensive behaviors do not work, a monitor lizard can bite. Some keepers are of the opinion that savannah and white-throated monitors readily tame down into compliant and docile animals that will not bite you. I have lived with some vicious animals that tail-whipped and bit me at every opportunity throughout their captivity, while other cagemates were as docile as could be.

In a lunge and bite, the monitor lizard lunges at the threat (you), sometimes in an airborne maneuver, bites said threat (you), and with typical monitor lizard tenacity, holds on. A monitor bite is a painful affair; its teeth are often sharp and are designed for lacerating and crushing.

Experienced keepers will tell you not to pull away from the lizard's grip when you do get bitten, as this can cause further damage to both you and the monitor. It can damage the monitor's mouth and teeth, and pulling away can cause you further tissue damage. Not pulling away from a monitor lizard that is biting you is a very difficult thing to do! Sometimes, applying bitter apple spray or even strong liquor in small amounts to the site where the monitor is attached may cause it to release you. When handling a monitor, especially one with a nasty disposition, it is always best to have someone with you, so if you are bitten, there is someone there who can help you with first aid. For first time keepers, being bitten by even a moderately sized monitor lizard can be a traumatic event.

If you should be bitten, depending on the severity of the bite, medical attention may be necessary. If you visit a doctor about your encounter, provide your physician with information about the species, its size, and the time of the bite. Have someone go with you to the doctor and/or hospital when medical attention is required, because monitor bites may appear minor but can be serious. If the bite is minor, wash it out and apply some antibiotic ointment and a bandage. Keep an eye on it for signs of infection. Once savannah and white-throated monitors become tame, they are unlikely to bite. Savannahs in particular are often described as "dog tame."

Another defensive behavior of monitors is expanding the throat. Wise keepers heed their monitors' warning signals.

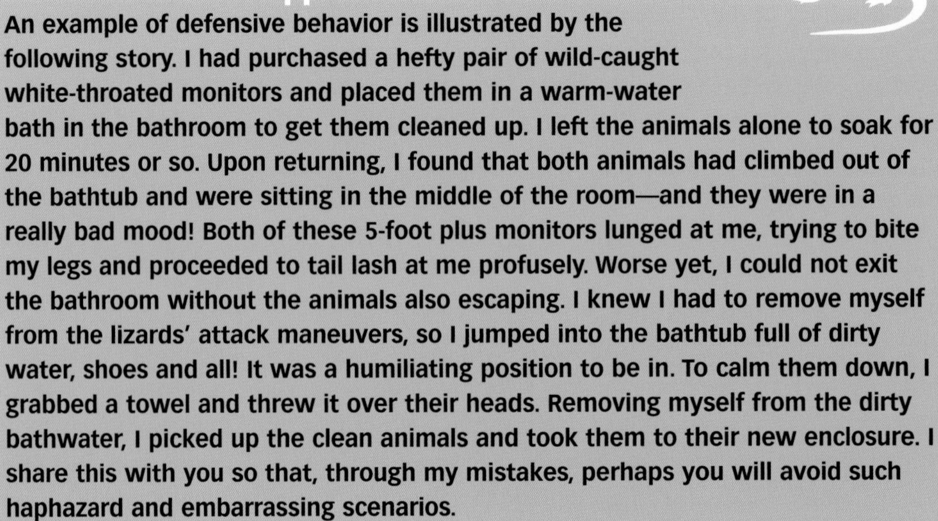

Don't Let This Happen To You

An example of defensive behavior is illustrated by the following story. I had purchased a hefty pair of wild-caught white-throated monitors and placed them in a warm-water bath in the bathroom to get them cleaned up. I left the animals alone to soak for 20 minutes or so. Upon returning, I found that both animals had climbed out of the bathtub and were sitting in the middle of the room—and they were in a really bad mood! Both of these 5-foot plus monitors lunged at me, trying to bite my legs and proceeded to tail lash at me profusely. Worse yet, I could not exit the bathroom without the animals also escaping. I knew I had to remove myself from the lizards' attack maneuvers, so I jumped into the bathtub full of dirty water, shoes and all! It was a humiliating position to be in. To calm them down, I grabbed a towel and threw it over their heads. Removing myself from the dirty bathwater, I picked up the clean animals and took them to their new enclosure. I share this with you so that, through my mistakes, perhaps you will avoid such haphazard and embarrassing scenarios.

Cloacal Evacuation

Following the hiss, tail-whip, and bite defenses, this next behavior is a most caustic one. Monitor lizards under duress or stress will very effectively evacuate their cloacal contents upon your person with amazing force; they can also evacuate with accuracy (they can aim their feces). When you have been the target of this chemical warfare tactic, gently and securely return your monitor lizard to its enclosure and lock it before changing your clothes. Always be on guard for this defensive behavior by pointing the cloaca away from yourself when handling a monitor.

Vomiting

Now this is truly a vile act of chemical warfare that any keeper wants to avoid. Although a monitor lizard can perpetrate defensive vomiting at any time, it most often occurs when the animals are in new and unfamiliar surroundings that have unknown noises and smells, which causes them a great deal of stress. In most instances, vomiting occurs when the keeper handles the monitor too soon after feeding, or if he startles it from a deep sleep perhaps following a large meal or when ambient temperatures decrease.

All of these defensive behaviors may seem intimidating; just remember that most savannah, white-throated, and eyed monitors settle down after a few weeks and will no longer feel threatened by their keeper.

Looping Behavior

When animals are threatened, some are able to trick their predators by playing dead, or "playing possum." Like the opossum, several species of monitor lizard also do this in their effort to escape possible predators.

Savannah monitors display two distinct forms of playing possum behavior. In one such display, they flip over onto their backs, bite their hind foot, and hold it. After observing this display, South African herpetologist Walter Rose called it "looping." This looping habit appeared to be a defense mechanism against predatory snakes because it would place a savannah monitor into a loop that was too large to ingest. Among monitor lizards, only the Bosc's monitor has been observed exhibiting looping behavior.

The white-throated monitor (*Varanus albigularis*) also displays playing possum behavior, but not as dramatically as the Bosc's monitor's looping. It simply goes limp, and its tongue may even hang out. This form of playing possum is called *tonic immobility*, which is triggered when vast amounts of adrenaline enter the animal's bloodstream.

Although savannah and white-throated monitors are often quite tame, any monitor will bite if it feels threatened.

Chapter 3

Purchasing a Savannah Monitor

It is always best to research your next pet before you go out and purchase it, but this seldom happens. This is the reason many monitor lizards are abandoned or given away—the owner simply did not know what he or she was getting into. Additionally, it is best to have your future pet's housing all set up before you bring the monitor home. This avoids having your monitor sit around in a cardboard box while you scramble to rig up lights and hide boxes.

Monitor Addiction

Many keepers go through a phase of rapidly acquiring monitors. For those hobbyists, keeping monitor lizards is analogous to any addiction: once you get one, you have to get two, then three, and so on. I have seen this happen not only to me, but to dozens of herp hobbyists. It is the nature of the *varanophile*—persons that love monitor lizards (*varanophile* is a term created by the editor of *VaraNews*, a monitor lizard newsletter created by Greg Nalcerio of Los Angeles, California).

If you are not careful, your home or apartment may become filled with wall-to-wall terraria housing monitor lizards of every size and species. Eventually, your collection will dwindle down to a more manageable number of animals. Don't worry, you are not alone; we have all gone through this. I think the excitement and wonderment about these animals causes us to do this, at least in the beginning stages of varanophilia. It is, of course, best to avoid this, because when the number of animals overextends the keeper, the care of those animals inevitably suffers.

Before Buying

Before purchasing a monitor lizard—savannah or any other kind—it is best to read all you can about the animal. Next, have your terrarium set up and ready to go, and then locate a few good reptile breeders.

It is a good idea to know what monitor you want before visiting a breeder or a reputable pet shop—a juvenile savannah monitor, an adult white-throated monitor, etc. In this way, any time spent looking at the animals and speaking with vendors will be to your greater advantage. But if you are not sure yet, that's alright. Looking around a good pet shop is fun, too.

When buying a monitor lizard, it is best to go to a pet shop that specializes in reptiles. Take a tour and note how the

Before purchasing a monitor, be sure you fully understand all of its care requirements and are willing to provide them.

animals are cared for. How clean is the store? Is there water in each water bowl in the terraria on the display floor? Do the animals appear alert and active? If you see that a few or more animals are sick, listless, or in filthy conditions, go to another pet shop. Do not buy a sick animal. Once you have looked around and seen that conditions are acceptable, ask if you can speak with someone who specializes in monitor lizards, and ask questions about the animal you are interested in purchasing. When you are satisfied that a particular pet shop meets necessary standards and the animals within it are healthy, proceed to the next step.

Another source of monitors is the reptile expo (also called herp expos, reptile shows, and swap meets). These events take place at locations around the US fairly frequently. You can find them through the Internet, reptile publications, and local newspapers. At herp expos, you will find numerous vendors selling many species of reptiles, amphibians, and possibly tarantulas, along with a wide range of food and supplies. Some of those vendors will certainly be selling Bosc's and/or white-throated monitors. The benefit of these shows is that you usually can inspect a number of lizards from at least a few different vendors.

Before You Get a Savannah Monitor

You should have all the necessary lizard-keeping supplies and equipment on-hand before you actually acquire the lizard itself. Here's a quick list of the needed items:

- **an appropriately sized cage**
- **the correct heating and lighting equipment**
- **the right food**
- **safe and appropriate climbing branches and hide boxes**
- **realistic expectations of what life with a monitor lizard is like**

Selecting a Healthy Monitor

Once you have seen a monitor that you like, look at it carefully. You are looking for signs of good or ill health.

Are the eyes clear and wide open? If the eyes seem dull or unresponsive, this is not the animal you want to take home with you. Does the monitor look at you when you approach the terrarium? Does it puff up when the clerk opens the enclosure, or does it just lay there? Ask the clerk when it was last given food and what it was fed. Ask him or her to offer the animal some food and see how it reacts. Does it eat in front of you?

If the clerk's answers satisfy you, and the animal looks and acts healthy, great! If you do

Starting with a young savannah or white-throat increases your chance of having a tame adult monitor.

not like the animals on display, ask if they have any animals off-display that you can see. The monitor lizard should be alert, even aggressive, and attempting to bite. It might even defecate when being handled, which is fine because this shows that the animal is eating and behaving naturally.

If you have held monitor lizards before, ask the clerk if you can hold this particular animal. Monitors should be held firmly but not squeezed. They should be held behind the neck and in front of the forelegs with one hand, and with larger specimens, held firmly in front of the rear legs as well, with the tail held under your armpit so it cannot tail-whip you. If you do not want to handle it, you can simply place it on the floor. Examine the animal for activity, aggression, how it walks—is it walking aloft over the ground (good) or pulling itself along the floor like a slug (bad)? All of these aspects are good indicators of the animal's health.

Avoid Sick Lizards

It may be highly tempting to buy an obviously sick savannah monitor in hopes of saving it, but don't do it. Purchasing a sick monitor in order to rehabilitate it almost always ends with the lizard dead, your bank account smaller, and your heart broken. It is very difficult to rehabilitate a sick monitor.

The lizard may open its mouth, and if it does, examine its teeth and gums. A healthy specimen should have pink gums, sometimes with a dark patch of skin pigmentation on the insides of the mouth and throat regions. Inspect the gums and teeth for a cheesy-like substance known as stomatitis, or mouth rot, which is a common infection seen in many captive animals that are maintained at cooler temperatures in often unsanitary conditions. Do not choose any animal that has stomatitis. It can be difficult to treat.

Check the toenails for stiffness; if the nails are pliable and soft, the animal may have a malnutrition malady. Examine the lizard for exterior parasites such as ticks or mites, which frequent the nostrils, armpits, cloaca, and tail-base regions. Mites are very small red-colored animals that hide in folds of skin. If there is waste in the terrarium, look for pinworms and tapeworms.

Captive Bred Is Better

Although finding captive-bred savannah, white-throated, and eyed monitors is not easy, it always best to buy captive-bred monitors when possible. Captive-bred lizards are overall healthier than wild-caught ones, because they usually do not have parasites and have not been subjected to the stress of capture, transport, and holding. Also, these lizards are already adapted to life as a pet.

If the animal is listless, droopy, feels mushy, or the tail is limp and not firm to the touch, it is not well and should not be purchased. Whether you obtain a monitor lizard from a pet shop, a herpetology meeting, or show, the same guidelines for selecting a healthy lizard apply.

When you have chosen the monitor lizard you want to purchase, tell the clerk you are ready to make the sale. It is highly recommended that you go home and put your monitor in its new home right away. If you leave your monitor in the car for any length of time, it may overheat or, in cold weather, it could become too cold; either situation could kill your monitor. If you are ready to take you new pet home, the clerk will place the lizard in a cloth or paper bag or in a box. You could also bring your own container. Coolers work well (without the ice, obviously), as do cat carriers for larger individuals. No matter what type of container you use, it should be secure. Once you take the lizard to your car, put it on the floor in a shady place and not in direct sunlight (but not in the trunk!). Again, direct sunlight can overheat your animal and kill it before you get home. You have now taken the big step and are ready to experience the many joys of living with a monitor lizard. Congratulations and welcome to the world of the varanophile!

Chapter 4

Housing and Handling

Proper housing is essential to the well-being of a monitor lizard in captivity. The cage or terrarium size and type you choose will depend wholly on what kind of monitor you buy. For example, an enclosure for hatchlings will be different than one for subadults or adults. The contents of the enclosure will also be determined by the type and size of your monitor lizard.

Quarantine

It is always important to keep a newly purchased animal away from any other reptiles in your collection for several weeks. Keeping your new lizard in quarantine is important for both the animal and you. In this way, any illness or parasites it may have can be detected and then treated by your veterinarian. Some people may expect that because the pet shop they purchased their animal from was clean, the animal is also clean and healthy—this may not always be the case. Even a captive-bred reptile can have parasites; it could've been exposed to an infested animal before you bought it.

As an example of the importance of quarantine, here is a personal experience. In 1995, I brought a small savannah monitor home from a herp meeting and placed it into the quarantine terrarium set aside for newcomers. The young monitor appeared healthy, had clear eyes, ate well, and was fine for two days. On the third day, I found a horrible sight: The young monitor was on its back, legs aloft, dead. There was blood everywhere, all over the lizard, the glass, with no evidence of wounds of any kind. The blood seemed to have come from the animal's mouth. Sadly, I properly disposed of it. Within 48 hours, all of my adult savannah monitors and white-throated monitors were also dead. It was later suspected that a virus had been introduced by the young savannah in quarantine, perhaps resulting in a pulmonary embolism. It was

It is important to quarantine a newly purchased monitor for a few weeks, especially if you have other reptiles.

Southern Aquatics

Southern Aquatics Poole
BH17 7XZ
MID: **********15710
TID: ****0539
Visa debit
Card no: ************8201
PAN seq. no: 01
AID: A0000000031010
Sale
Amount: £5.00
Total: £5.00
APPROVED
Date & time: 07/06/2023 16:04
Auth code: 586447
Payment method: Chip
Verification method: Pin
Transaction ID: 522fe

a specific viral agent that killed my African monitors, but did not harm my Australian and Pacific monitors in the slightest. I had no physical contact with this young savannah monitor as I wore gloves and washed my hands before and after entering its cage.

It is always advisable to quarantine new animals, regardless of where they come from, and, if possible, keep them in separate rooms from where your established animals live. Always perform maintenance duties on the quarantined animal after completing chores on your established animals. Never use supplies (hide boxes, cleaning sponges, etc.) from the quarantine cage in the cages of your other animals.

Quarantine Tip

In the quarantine enclosure, newspaper may be the best substrate. It can be changed every day, so you can keep the cage clean easily. Also, the paper allows you to examine the feces for signs of ill health, and mites are visible on it.

Setting Up Your Terrarium

With reptiles, the location of the terraria is very important in maintaining appropriate habitat conditions. Try to avoid placing cages directly on the floor, as the floor is colder than the ambient air temperature just six inches above them. Do not place your enclosure near windows. On hot days, the terraria get hotter, and on cold days, the reverse is true. Make sure that you place elevated terraria on a sturdy table, and when necessary, bolt your enclosures to the table and/or walls.

It is also important to consider the animal's innate survival instinct. If you place an enclosure on the floor, the monitor lizard sees only your feet and has little perception of how big you are. In nature, the smaller an animal is, the more likely larger animals will eat it, hence its instinct is to run and hide from predators. With this in mind, place smaller enclosures at chest to waist level, so that you are not as intimidating to the monitors. As they grow in size and become accustomed to you, they lose this innate fear and become more docile; they learn to tolerate you and understand you are not a threat to them.

As the animals grow larger, you can move your terraria closer to the floor. For white-throated monitors or other semi-arboreal lizards, it's a good idea to place the enclosures higher, giving them the perception that they are above you or are larger than you are, which will make them feel more secure and less stressed. You can measure their stress levels by seeing how active they are during daylight hours. Stressed animals will hide, feed, dig, and

Cage Before Lizard

Have the terrarium set up and waiting for your new monitor lizard before you bring it home. This minimizes its stress and the time it spends in a cold, uncomfortable box.

bask less than unstressed animals. So watch your animals, and let them tell you how they feel. Males are more active than the more sedentary females, but both sexes should be active daily unless they are hibernating or aestivating.

The home range of an average wild white-throated monitor male is about 7-15 square miles (11.3-24.1 sq km) and for females about 3.5-8 square miles (4.8-9.3 sq km) (Albert, 1994; Phillips, 1995, Lemm, 1996, 1998). So, offering your adult monitor the largest enclosure possible is recommended. Large enclosures are better for offering temperature ranges, exercise, and giving the lizard more ground to investigate on its daily regimen of foraging, exploring, and digging (for food, burrows, boredom). The larger the enclosure, the more behaviors it will exhibit, the healthier it is likely to be, and with luck, the longer its life will be. Because the monitors we are discussing are avid diggers and climbers, offer your monitor as long, wide, and tall an enclosure as possible. When purchasing or constructing your lizard's enclosure, provide a cage that is at least two times the total length of your monitor lizard in all dimensions.

Glass Terraria

Glass terraria are good for smaller, younger monitor lizards. A larger enclosure causes them to feel too exposed and is not reflective of a hatchling's "home range," which is quite small. However, the terrarium should be no smaller than 20-gallons (75.7 l) for a proper temperature gradient to exist. Also, be sure it is properly sealed and waterproof. Of course, when your monitor has outgrown the enclosure, you can move it into a larger wooden enclosure.

Maintaining proper temperature is essential in any enclosure. The larger your glass terrarium is, the more heat it will require to remain sufficiently warm. Because it has glass walls, it does not hold heat very well. To slow down heat loss, place construction paper on three sides of the enclosure, keeping one side uncovered. This offers the smaller monitor lizard a sense of security while reducing stress and enables it to feel comfortable enough to venture out of its hide spots to investigate its environment.

There are drawbacks to using a glass terrarium. It is heavy and can easily break. Also, heat lamps can only be applied from above. Most aquariums have screen tops that allow all of the

Glass aquaria are often used for savannah monitors, but they are not the best choice for an enclosure.

heat and humidity to escape, a situation you want to avoid. Also, be aware that heat sources for aquariums do not usually offer an adequate temperature range for reptiles. Although a Plexiglas terrarium can be used, it tends to scratch easily and becomes visually unappealing to the keeper. Tops for many Plexiglas terraria are not suitable for monitor lizards, as they often easily escape from such enclosures.

Appropriate tops for enclosures are one of the most important items for any reptile-oriented habitat. If the top has holes in it for ventilation, warm air can leave the enclosure, bringing it to room temperature. Therefore, it's always better to use a solid top cover and put screening materials on the sides. With glass terraria, make sure tops are fastened down tightly with clamps; if not, a monitor will surely find a way out of its cage! Do not pile books, food, equipment, or clothing on top of the terrarium, because these tops may be hot and anything flammable may catch fire. Also, most wire-mesh and wooden tops are not designed to have prolonged weight on them and can weaken or even break, creating an avalanche of junk that falls on top of your monitor lizard, possibly crushing it.

Plan Ahead

Remember that monitor lizards grow fast. So, if you start with a juvenile, you might want to go directly from a small or medium sized enclosure to its final, large sized adult cage, rather than purchasing cage after cage for each stage of the lizard's growing life. It can get expensive otherwise.

Wooden Terraria

In many ways, wooden terraria are better to use than glass terraria. They are better at holding in heat. They also provide a more secure place for younger animals because they are only exposed to viewing from the front. Most wooden enclosures have doors that open from the front or sides, as

Custom-made wooden enclosures are superior to glass aquaria in many ways. They hold heat better and are easier to access for cleaning, for example.

opposed to only top entry in glass terraria. Wooden enclosures can be built to any size and specification for less money than a glass enclosure of equal size. The keeper can even apply personal touches to the enclosures, such as placing wooden lattice structures within the enclosure nailed to the walls. This provides the monitor with something to climb, which encourages much needed exercise.

Molded Plastic Enclosures

Although molded plastic cages appear to work for snakes, they are not really adequate or proper for monitor lizards. The sliding doors of this type of enclosure can be opened by a monitor, and many monitors will

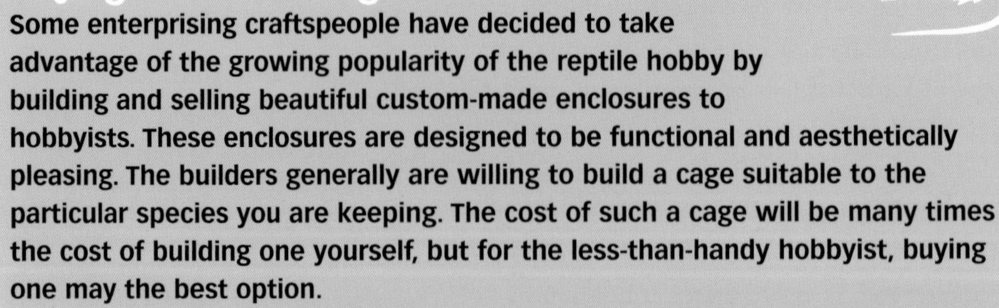

Buying a Custom Cage

Some enterprising craftspeople have decided to take advantage of the growing popularity of the reptile hobby by building and selling beautiful custom-made enclosures to hobbyists. These enclosures are designed to be functional and aesthetically pleasing. The builders generally are willing to build a cage suitable to the particular species you are keeping. The cost of such a cage will be many times the cost of building one yourself, but for the less-than-handy hobbyist, buying one may the best option.

Companies and individuals that custom-make reptile cages can be found at herp expos, in reptile related publications, and on the Internet. You can also contact a local carpenter and find out if he or she would be able to build a cage to suit your needs.

learn to open them. Because these cages are made of plastic and monitor lizards require heat, the heat sources can singe, melt, and burn the plastic terrarium. Burning plastic releases toxic fumes, so for this reason alone, these type of enclosures should be avoided. Furthermore, most of these enclosures are not tall enough for these species.

Outdoor Enclosures

Outdoor enclosures are, of course, the most preferred habitat, but due to size constraints are a rare sight for the private keeper. Most zoos have outdoor enclosures for many of their monitor lizards, with adjacent indoor enclosures as well. This would be the optimal terrarium choice for any captive monitor.

Building an outdoor enclosure is beyond the scope of this book. However, here are some pointers in case you decide to build one. You must sink the walls of the enclosure into the ground at least 18 inches (46 cm) to prevent your monitor from digging under it. The height of the walls above ground should be at least twice as tall as your monitor is long (total length including tail). Most local predators—cats, dogs, hawks, etc.—will leave a full-grown savannah or white-throated monitor alone. If you are housing juveniles outside, you will have to make sure your enclosure is predator-proof. Fencing in your yard is a good idea,

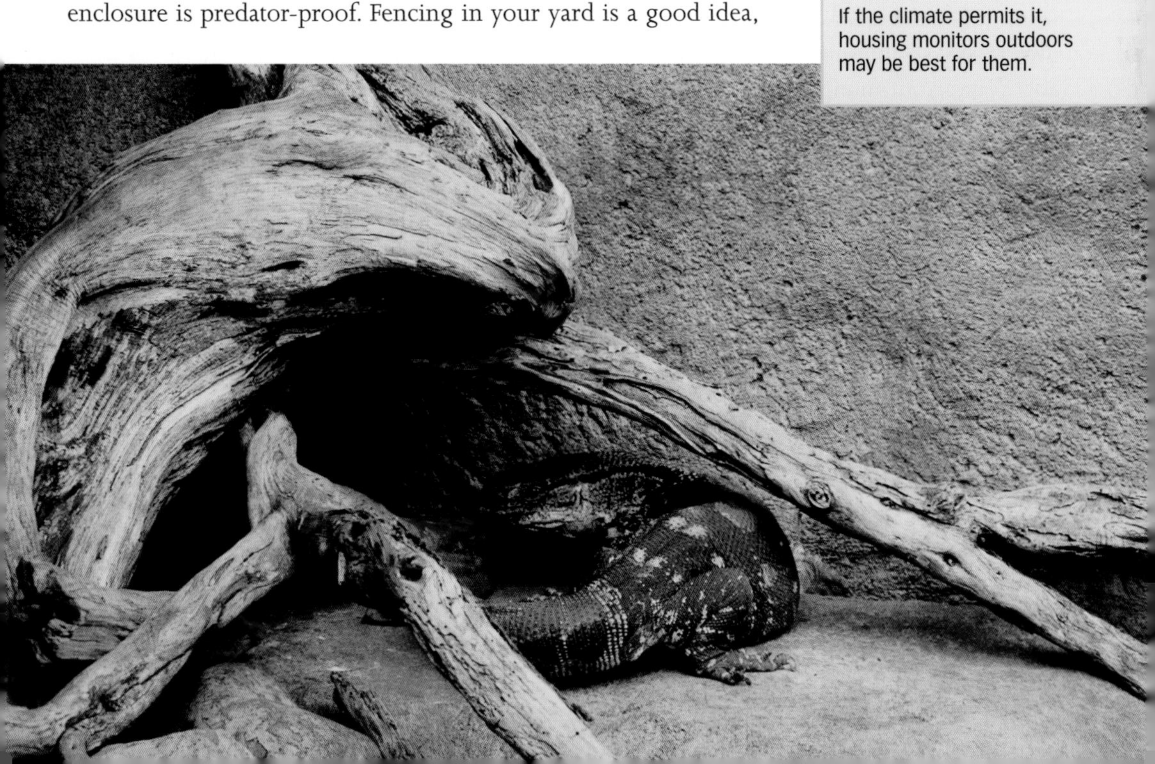

If the climate permits it, housing monitors outdoors may be best for them.

in case your monitor does escape. The fence will provide a secondary level of containment. Last, you must make sure that monitors in outdoor enclosures always have fresh water and access to both basking areas and shady retreats.

Lights

Lights and heating elements should be on the inside of your enclosure, at least 18 inches (45.7 cm) above the highest object within it. If possible, use multiple low-watt porcelain light sockets because they reduce the possibility of fire. Lights should be encased in a metal screen light socket protector or light guard that can be screwed into the enclosure; monitor lizards tend to cling to unprotected lights and can burn themselves. Using multiple low-watt bulbs also allows your monitor to attain the thermoregulatory temperatures it requires, and the heat generated from these bulbs is not enough to burn your animals.

Incandescent lights are the most common method for heating savannah monitors.

Some people advocate keeping reptile lights on 24 hours a day, 7 days a week. This is not advisable for your African monitor lizard. These animals need sleep, which means the enclosure needs to be dark. As anyone knows, sleeping during the heat and light of the day is difficult. Turn your lights off every night. Monitor lizards can have a photoperiod of 12 hours of light and 12 hours of darkness. If you are concerned about temperatures during the night, you can add a red or blue colored bulb, which has longer wavelengths, does not interfere with their sleep periods, and will provide heat. Ceramic heat emitters are another option for nighttime heating. These are bulb-like items that generate heat but not light.

For African monitors, the summer months (September to February) are their reproductive and aestivation season, so increase the photoperiod to 14 hours per day to simulate their natural environment and induce natural behaviors. Having a timer to control the photoperiod is highly recommended.

There is a plethora of opinions as to which light sources are good and not good for reptiles; entire books could be written on this subject alone. Sunlight is the best heat and light source for reptiles, but it's not always practical for the keeper to use sunlight. So what is a good substitute for natural sunlight? I use normal incandescent bulbs, with seasonal natural sunlight exposure whenever possible. There are bulbs said to duplicate the sunlight spectrum. Avoid black lights (ultraviolet A) as they emit long wavelengths dangerous to the eye and, with constant exposure, can cause blindness. Never look directly into a black light bulb. I know keepers who kept their monitor lizards under such bulbs, and those particular animals became blind. A coincidence? Perhaps, but not likely.

Ultraviolet B (UVB) light is said to promote vitamin D3 synthesis in reptiles. Some lizards utilize UVB light for D3 synthesis better than others. Some require light more than dietary D3, and visa versa. Monitor lizards appear to be better at metabolizing dietary vitamin D3 from sunlight. This suggests they rely more on dietary uptakes for their calcium needs than herbivorous reptiles that rely more on sunlight for this requirement.

Careful Heating

Many monitor lizards get burned by lights that are too close or too intense in radiant heat (high-wattage bulbs) while basking. The substrate can also become too hot and cause thermal burns on their feet and belly. To avoid this, take periodic readings of the ambient air, basking sites, and cool side to check that temperatures are adequate and that a good temperature gradient exists within the enclosure. Using a thermostat on your heating equipment is highly recommended. Burns are extremely painful for reptiles and mammals alike! If your monitor should receive burns, take it to a veterinarian immediately.

Temperature and Heating

The author has read online forums in which people advise keeping monitor lizards at temperatures ranging from 130°-150°F (54.4°-65.6°C). At 107°F (76.7°C), animal tissue rapidly dehydrates. At 129°F (53.9°C) proteins begin to break down within living

Behavioral Thermoregulation

Because monitors and other reptiles have no way of controlling their temperature physiologically, they use various behaviors to do the job. This is called behavioral thermoregulation, which simply means controlling temperature through behavior. For monitors, behavioral thermoregulation involves moving in and out of the sunlight as they get too hot or too cool. The keeper needs to be aware of behavioral thermoregulation in order to set up a proper captive environment. The monitor must be given a range of temperatures in his enclosure, so it can select the temperature it prefers at a given moment.

organisms. Is it wise to keep your animal(s) at such high ambient temperatures? Can it be detrimental to their health and welfare? So why do some people keep their reptiles at such high temperatures? Because someone told them to! Basking temperatures of 105°F (40.6°C) should be sufficient for proper thermoregulation of healthy animals; health can be determined, in part, by their behaviors.

In captivity, it is critical to provide your monitor with opportunities to control its own temperatures. Provide a hot side and a cool side in your enclosure, with a 20°F (-6.7°C) degree temperature gradient, but do not make it too hot or too cold for it to live comfortably! Place a hide spot on each side of the enclosure so that your monitor may thermoregulate. This allows your monitor ever greater control of its internal temperature and doesn't force it to choose between feeling secure and being at its preferred temperature.

To know if the temperatures are right for your monitor, watch it. If it spends most of its time under the heat lamps or on the hot side, then your enclosure might be too cold and will require additional heat. If your monitor spends too much of its time on the cooler end, then your enclosure is probably too hot and may require a decrease of heating elements. Sometimes determining its comfort zones is simple when you let the animal help you figure out what is best for it.

Begin keeping your terrarium or enclosure at an ambient air temperature of about 95°F (34.9°C) and see where your monitor lizard spends most of its time during a 72-hour period. Make adjustments to the temperature by changing lamp wattage intensities or by changing the elevation of the lamps as you see fit until your animal seems to spend an adequate amount of time basking and engaging in other activities in the enclosure. A monitor that spends a majority of its time basking or staying at the far end of the enclosure is not being provided with an adequate thermal gradient within its terrarium. So observe your monitor, and let it tell you what it needs.

Humidity

Humidity is a necessary component of your monitor lizard's well-being. It can increase the ambient air temperature of an enclosure without further heat output, it helps the animal with skin shedding, and it can help hatchlings with hydration. Dehydration is the hatchling's greatest enemy and can cause death. If you live in a dry area where humidity levels are low year-round, you can purchase a humidifier at most hardware and drug stores. A humidifier increases water moisture in the air. Purchase an ultrasonic humidifier, not a hot or cold humidifier.

Fluctuations in humidity can cause skin problems. If a lizard's skin is kept too moist, shed skin can stick to its body, causing constriction, especially around toes and ankles. I have seen constriction by shed skin around a young savannah monitor's neck, too.

Comfortable humidity levels for the African monitor lizard can be low to moderate; 20-50 percent is fine. During the summer months in Africa (September to February), humidity levels around 50 percent appear to promote courtship behavior (Williams, pers. obs.).

White-throated, savannah, and eyed monitors are from dry areas of Africa, so they only require moderate humidity in their enclosures.

Ventilation

Ventilation is needed to make conditions in your terrarium suitable (as you will learn when your monitor evacuates). Tiny ventilation holes, a fine screen mesh, or a vented screen on the sides of the enclosure are recommended. Do not place ventilation holes on the top of your enclosure, as this will allow heat to escape into the room. Also, do not place fans or other mechanical devices inside of the enclosure, as most monitor lizards will investigate these devices using their tongues and can get them caught or pulled off.

Substrates

Substrates for monitor lizards are a hot topic. Lizards like to dig, so they need an appropriate substrate in their enclosures. Wild white-throated monitors dig their burrows and nests in dolerite koppies and, therefore, like to dig in dolomite substrates. Dolomite is a limestone deposit (calcium carbonate) and is readily available at many garden centers.

Soil Substrates

Garden variety top soil (not potting soil) mixed with clean sand is often used as a substrate, and it works well enough for subadult and adult animals, but it is not recommended for hatchlings because it is dusty and can dehydrate them, and it can be ingested by the little monitor. Soil ingested by a juvenile monitor can collect and cause intestinal impaction and even death. You can use this substrate for hatchlings, if you

Some keepers use sand as the substrate in their savannah and white-throated monitor enclosures.

pay careful attention to the humidity and feed them on a plate or in a bowl to prevent injestion of the soil.

Potting soil is often recommended, but after a few weeks can become moldy and rot. You do not want compost soil in wooden terraria. Some keepers mix equal parts of sand/dirt/sphagnum moss, which also works. The sphagnum moss soaks up any moisture in the substrate, the sand allows for compaction of the substrate medium, and the dirt acts like glue binding the three components together. The only drawback to such a mixed substrate is that it is a heavy medium to add and remove from your enclosures. Some keepers use only sand, but it is still very heavy, and for burrows, only works when wet.

Leaf Litter

The best substrate medium is simple, lightweight, and usually free. Go to your neighborhood or local city park and find oak trees (*Quercus* sp.), and if necessary, ask someone if you may collect the leaves deposited on the ground. Bring lots of trash bags with you, and load up! The oak leaves act as a natural scent remover in your enclosure, they provide a deep substrate for digging, exploring, and foraging, and they are easy

The author prefers to use leaf litter as the substrate in his monitor enclosures.

Inappropriate Substrates

Here is a short list of substrates you should never use in an African monitor enclosure:

- **artificial turf**
- **bare floor**
- **bark chips**
- **gravel**
- **pine or cedar shavings**
- **reptile carpet-type substrates**

to remove and throw away. It is a free, renewable resource. You can't beat that! For burrows, bury a plastic or wooden box with soil in it under the leaf litter and see how the animals react to it.

Assessing Your Substrate

Watch your monitor and see if it is doing alright with the substrate. Is it digging? Is it exploring? If not, check the heat and hydration. If those variables are okay, then perhaps something is wrong with the substrate, or your monitor lizard may be ill. Let you lizard tell you how it feels by watching it—which is terrific fun, in any case.

Avoid pine shavings and wood chips, because minute pieces can lodge in the eyes or cloacae or be ingested by younger monitor lizards while they explore, dig, feed, and defecate. Wood chips lodged in an orifice will probably require a visit to your veterinarian, who will have to remove the obstruction.

Some people use newspaper and/or recycled paper bedding as a substrate. There is nothing wrong with using these substrates—except when they are wet and remain so for a prolonged period, they become a mess. Also, a monitor cannot dig into newspaper as one can dig through a soil, sand, or oak-leaf substrate.

Water

A large and sturdy water bowl is a necessary fixture in an African monitor enclosure. Ambient temperature is crucial for your monitor lizard. If ambient air temperature is high, your monitor may need to cool down quickly, and that means a soak in the water basin. So provide an ample-sized water basin your animal can fit his entire body into, one that will allow him to fully soak to cool down and properly thermoregulate. It is a good idea to show your monitor where the water bowl is when you first introduce it to the enclosure.

If your monitor spends too much time in its water bowl, the enclosure may be too hot or you may have insufficient hide spots for it to retreat to. Always watch your lizard, use some common sense, and have fun figuring out what it is telling you with its actions. Sometimes, actions speak louder than words.

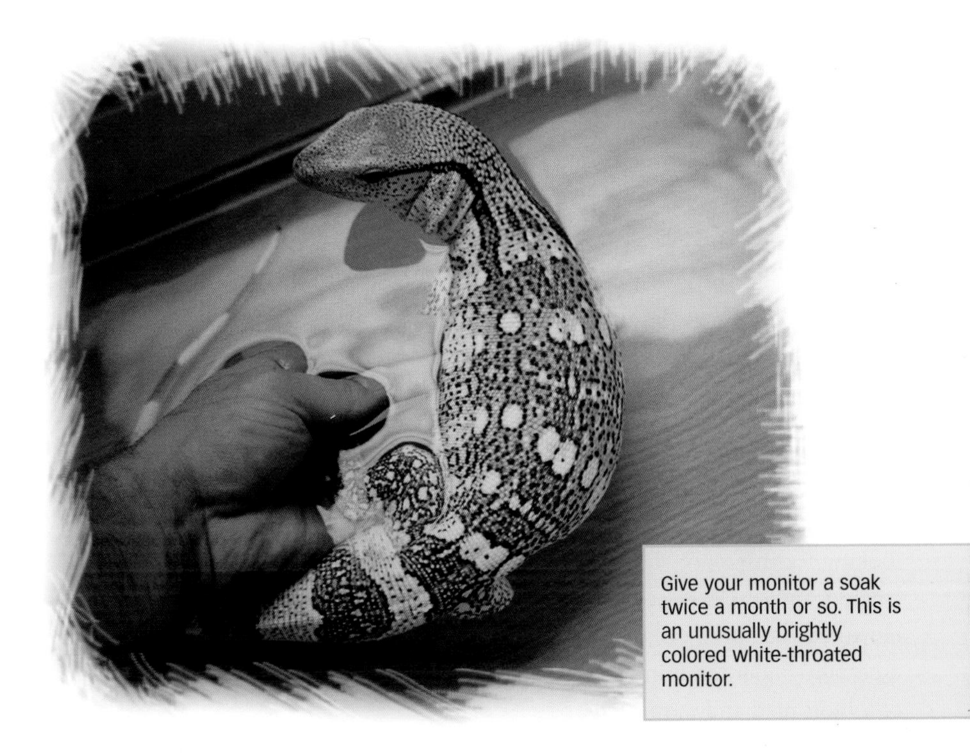

Give your monitor a soak twice a month or so. This is an unusually brightly colored white-throated monitor.

The white-throated monitor is not fond of water and may resist your intentions to place it into a bathtub or pool of water. Once in there, it may inflate its body cavity with air and sulk. Keep an eye on it, so it does not crawl out and cause trouble by hiding in your linen, etc. A wet white-throated monitor will tail lash you just as effectively as a dry one, so beware of this when removing your monitor from the bathtub/water basin.

When removing a (tame) monitor lizard from the bathtub, especially if it is a big one, beware of the tail-lashing abilities and splashing this can elicit. Grab big lizards by the neck with one hand, and then gently scoop your other hand under their tail base bringing your arm under the body and using it as a platform.

When placing your animal into a bathtub, kiddy pool, etc., be sure the water is not hot or cold, but warm. When giving a monitor lizard a bath, always make sure the toilet seat and lid are down, as you do not want a small monitor to escape via that route. Watch it as you would a small child when it plays in the water—attentively. I recommend soaking monitors for 30 to 45 minutes every two weeks or so. Do not allow the bath water to become chilled, as the monitor will also become cold. Afterwards, you should disinfect your tub with a solution of 5-10 percent bleach. Leave the bleach in the tub for at least 15 minutes before rinsing.

Rocks and Plants

Rocks and plants certainly make an enclosure look nice, but are they practical? Yes and no. They may be good for a hatchling monitor, which is a creature of curiosity that will explore every part of its enclosure all day long, especially looking for insects or shade in crevices and cracks between rocks. However, rock piles can easily fall, especially under the ministrations of a motivated and inquisitive monitor lizard. There is nothing sadder than coming home to find a baby monitor crushed under a rock, so use common sense and be practical when considering rocks. To prevent this, you can cement the stones together, which could work.

You can use a kiddie pool to soak larger monitors. Only soak your monitor outdoors on warm days.

Some people use stacks of wood or plastic boxes rather than stone, but these items can promote splinters and abrasions. If you do choose to use them, make sure they are sanded smooth. Also, wood platforms exposed to thermal gradients, humidity, etc., can become weakened, so be sure they are strong enough to support your lizard.

Monitor lizards love to dig, and if there are living plants in your enclosure, they will surely dig them up. If your enclosure is large enough, you

Climbing Tip

Lattice wood commonly used in garden trellises for roses and passion vines works well for allowing these lizards to climb around on the walls of their enclosure. You can affix it to the sides of the enclosure to give your monitors more usable climbing surfaces.

Although savannah and white-throated monitors are considered terrestrial, they will climb when given the opportunity.

can place live potted plants in it. Yes, they will dig, maybe even burrow, but the plants are a good place for crickets and similar prey to hide, and where monitor lizards can forage, which gives them the mental stimulation lacking in many terraria.

Plastic plants can also be used, but be aware that the leaves can become detached and small plastic pieces can be ingested. You do not want your monitor eating plastic. If you do use them, securely cement them together using nontoxic glue before including them in your enclosure.

Hide Spots

Most African monitors live in burrows, termite mounds, or rock crevices in the wild. (Phillips, 1995; Lemm, 1996, 1998; Bennett, 1998, 2000:304, 2003; Watt, 1999:48). Your monitor lizard's new home will need to recreate its natural habitat and include things like hiding areas. I have seen everything from a tissue box to paper towel tubes used for hide spots; these are not recommended because they become dirty and rot. Hide spots should be roomy enough for the animal to completely hide in, yet snug enough for sleeping. Hide spots can be plastic opaque boxes with bored out holes for entry and exit, bird houses (for

All monitors need some type of hiding area in order to feel secure and reduce stress. This one has created its own burrow.

smaller animals), rock piles, masonry bricks, hollowed bricks, wooden boxes, aquariums, cork bark, or man-made caves. I have even seen toy train tunnels used for hidespots, although they soon fall apart. Whatever you use for a hide spot, make sure it is sturdy and will not cave in or tip over and crush your monitor.

Provide your monitor with multiple hide spots, as lizards like to explore and take refuge in various hiding places. It may use all of the hide spots, or just one. The animal needs to feel secure.

Avoid violating the hide spot by lifting it, moving it, or shaking it. The hide spot is the monitor's home, and the sanctity of it should be respected. The monitor will soon use the hide spots as bases of operations. Face the openings toward a heat source, so they can heat up more quickly; in the wild, burrows often face east toward the sunrise. Your monitor lizard may bring its prey into the hide box and leave it there, so when you take your lizard out for bathing, a walk, etc., check hide spots for debris.

Bathroom Etiquette

Monitor lizards are messy. They produce an enormous amount of waste. Captive monitor lizards are prone to walk in their own feces, so it is recommended you remove their waste as soon as possible. Use a doggy bag, a toy shovel, or garden shovel to remove the waste. Avoid contact with your skin, as it is a source of bacteria, and always wash your hands before and after your sanitation duties.

Monitor lizards appear to choose where they excrete their waste. Sometimes it is in the water bowl or far away from their hide spots or basking sites, sometimes not, but they are usually consistent in where they defecate.

Cage Cleaning

Monitor lizards watch you clean their enclosures and seem to know what you are doing. Many a time I have observed my 6-foot (1.8 m) white-throat watch me clean her cage, carefully investigating what I was doing in her territory. She would intently watch me every time. I was able to use my bare hands without fear of them being interpreted as food because I never hand fed her.

Cage cleaning can be a labor-intensive task and is unpleasant to do, especially if it has been a few days since you have done so! All monitor feces should be removed from the enclosure and dumped into your compost heap or trash receptacle. Any fruit used as a food source for your feeder insects inside the enclosure should be removed to avoid generating fruit flies and gnats.

Paper-Trained Monitors?

You can paper train your monitor lizard. Place newspaper where your monitor lizard defecates. The lizard will defecate on it soon thereafter. Replace the newspaper every other day. After several weeks, move the newspaper to a new location and the lizards will defecate on it wherever it is placed. Who said monitor lizards were dumb?

Your substrate may require replacement once a month, bi-monthly, or every six months, depending on the substrate used. Changing the water and removing feces should be a daily affair. More intensive duties include substrate removal, glass cleaning, wall cleaning, and decoration cleaning. Use a diluted soap solution to clean the cage; submerge decorative pieces completely in a diluted bleach solution (a 5-10 percent solution) for at least 15 minutes and then rinse thoroughly. Let them bake outside in the sunlight for a day or more before returning them to the enclosure.

While you are cleaning the enclosure thoroughly, you can place your monitor lizard into a clean basin or trashcan for security, or give it a soak in the bathtub. Once you clean out the enclosure, the decorations, and so on, put the monitor back into its enclosure. Beware that if you shift monitors from one enclosure to another while cleaning, violence can occur because you have just placed a "foreigner" into another monitor's enclosure that has established this terrarium as its territory. It may attack the newcomer; I have seen this occur with savannah, white-throated, and Nile monitor lizards.

Escape

Many monitor lizards maintain their activity levels by seeking a way out of the box you have created for them. Trusted animals may be let out, so they can enjoy exploring your home—as long as you watch them very carefully. However, they can get stuck behind the refrigerator or crawl into a hole in the wall, and these scenarios can go from benign to nightmarish in seconds.

Monitors will explore every square inch of their enclosures for a way to escape. Glass is such a foreign object to them that they may be seen scratching at it or nose-rubbing on it for hours on end. A solution to this would be to place some masking tape on the bottom two inches of the windows, which would make them opaque and stop this behavior from occurring.

Should your monitor lizard escape, it probably won't venture very far. These animals generally stay near their enclosures, hidden somewhere in dark, tight-fitting places such as behind furniture, under a low table, in a closet, etc. If you do not find your lizard right away, place a bowl of water and perhaps some food out for it, so it does not dehydrate or go hungry. I had lost a savannah monitor for three weeks and figured it had escaped outside. One evening, I noticed a 2-foot (61 cm) long lizard turn the corner and walk into the

Most monitor lizards will take any opportunity to escape their cage and roam around. Always lock your monitor's cage.

Lock the Cage

Be sure all of your enclosures are securely locked with a key, as this will decrease the likelihood of unfortunate scenarios occurring, such as with small children who may haphazardly investigate this strange animal in a box. This can have serious ramifications, not only to your own family and friends, but with city, state, or federal officials. We have all seen bad press associated with such headlines like, "Baby Bitten by a Dragon," and these incidents fuel the fires of those who want to ban the keeping of reptiles. Not to mention, a child getting seriously injured by a monitor would be a tragic event. Be careful and be responsible.

bedroom! He looked healthy and fit. I picked it up easily and placed it back into its enclosure, where it remained. Where it had hidden, only the lizard knew.

It is imperative that your monitor never escape outside. Every time a reptile escapes it fuels the fires of those that want to ban the keeping of reptiles. It doesn't matter that a 3-foot (91 cm) savannah is not a threat to anyone; these people will claim it is dangerous to the community. Similarly, never take your monitor out in public, except in venues such as herp expos. Remember that you represent all herp keepers and act responsibly.

Activity Patterns, Burrows, and Sleep

Monitor lizards are primarily diurnal animals, which means they sleep at night. They generally awaken between 8 to 10 a.m., depending on the ambient temperature. They then move to their basking sites for 30-40 minutes to warm up before foraging for food and perhaps drink. From noon to 4 p.m., they seek shade and avoid the heat of the day, and then may resume their activities from 4 to 8 p.m., when they go to their hide spots and sleep.

Most monitor lizards sleep in their hide spots or burrows, and when climate conditions are adverse, they block the burrow with dirt. The burrow is usually at a constant temperature, depending on how deep and at what angle it is. I observed several savannah monitors collectively dig a three-chambered burrow 11 feet, 8 inches (3.6 m) at a 45-degree angle deep into the soil. Burrows allow animals to maintain optimal body temperatures, to properly thermoregulate, to retreat when threatened, and to sleep in safety (Bayless, 1994; Lenz, 1995:151-152; Blamires, 2001).

A leaf litter substrate allows the monitor to go underground, stay in the dark, cram itself

Because they are so intelligent, monitor lizards often become bored and depressed if not given enough stimulation.

into a nook or cranny, and sleep during the night. Some monitor lizards have been known to be active during warmer nights, often patrolling for food, or more likely for mates. When their nocturnal activities increase, especially for female monitor lizards, they are probably seeking out nesting sites.

Many captive animals become bored or depressed and listless while in captivity. This is a common enough scenario and can be easily corrected with terrarium alterations (Hediger, 1964, 1968; Jeungst, 1997; Labenda, 2001). If you have more than one animal in a small terrarium, separate them; stress or depression can result from dominant animals suppressing subordinate members within a terrarium causing them to become reclusive and sullen (Attum et al., 2001; Stanner, 1991; Pierson, pers. obs.). Bored animals can be rejuvenated by introducing new items into their enclosures, such as cork bark objects scented by another monitor (switch items from one monitor enclosure to another—as long as both monitors are healthy and parasite free). Adding wooden-lattice structures to terrarium walls or hollowed out structures for them to explore in which food can be hidden induces foraging behavior and curiosity. Add or remove cage items periodically while they are asleep. These simple things can improve the daily quality of life, and makes for healthier and more comfortable cohabitants in your home.

You may want to review other sources on monitor lizards; some of the sources on African monitor lizard natural history and husbandry, although brief, are very good. Check the References and Resources at the back of this book.

Handling

Avoid handling new arrivals, especially hatchlings. Handling induces stress, and as we know, stress is a silent killer. Leave new monitors alone for several weeks, keeping interactions to a minimum. After the animal seems more relaxed (ensuing in behaviors such as basking, feeding without running away, digging, etc.), begin hanging around it more often, letting it adjust to you and your presence in the same room.

If your monitor lizard tolerates you and does not attempt to hiss, bite, or tail lash, use your hand and arm to scoop up the lizard. Gently lift your monitor by scooping it from underneath the cloaca end toward its head end. Your arm will provide support for your lizard while it is being lifted. The monitor will hold onto your arm with its claws; this can cause some discomfort and scratching.

Monitor lizards, like big snakes, have a real fear of falling, which can kill them, and holding them in this way alleviates their fears. You can use gloves, but gloves can make it difficult to

Stress

Stress is a silent killer—present everywhere, seen nowhere. If one or more of your animals caged together seem listless, off-feed, and have their eyes shut, then perhaps stress is the cause. The easiest way to avoid combat and high stress levels between your monitor lizards is to keep them separated, or, failing that, provide enough space and multiple basking sites so each animal may bask comfortably and freely. Some of the other causes of stress include inadequate temperatures, lack of hiding areas, harassment by other pets (e.g. a cat sitting on top of the cage), and loud noises.

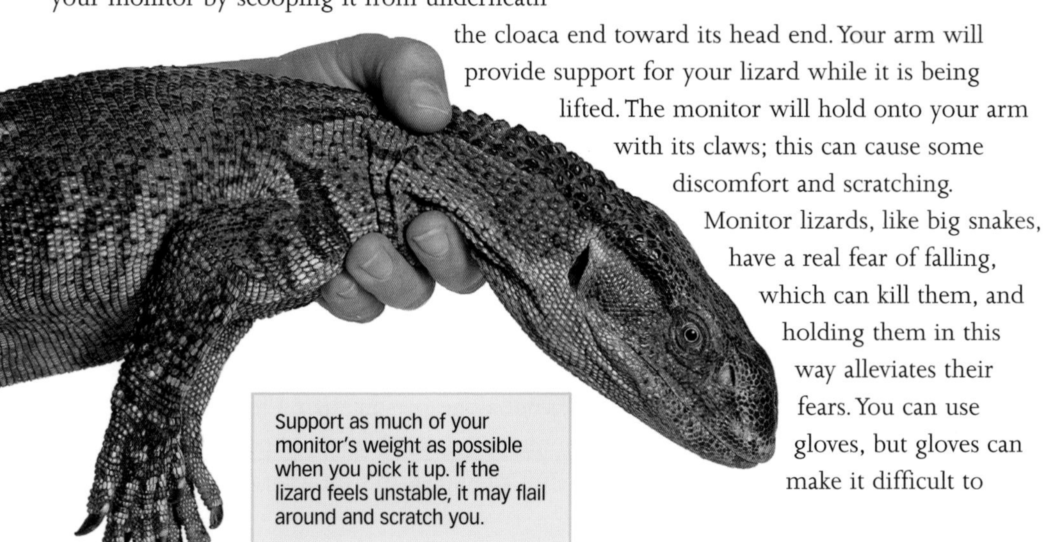

Support as much of your monitor's weight as possible when you pick it up. If the lizard feels unstable, it may flail around and scratch you.

Salmonella Risks

As with all reptiles, there is the possibility of contracting a *Salmonella* bacterial infection (salmonellosis) from lizards. This can result in severe gastric distress and diarrhea and—in rare cases—can be fatal. Anyone who handles reptiles should always thoroughly wash their hands before and afterwards and never eat or drink when handling a monitor. Although there is some risk of getting salmonellosis from your lizard and you should take precautions against contracting it, remember to put the risk in perspective. There is probably more risk of getting salmonellosis from eating chicken and eggs as there is from handling your lizard.

manipulate your monitor should it decide to run or escape your grasp.

With your free hand hold the monitor lizard's neck area, but do not squeeze tightly because you can injure it. The hyoid bones in the neck can be broken, causing strangulation of the animal. If you improperly handle your monitor, you can even dislocate its hips (hip luxation), so be careful. Firm yet gentle handling is a learned skill for both the keeper and the kept (Boyer, 1997).

For larger, aggressive monitor lizards, grab the monitor around the neck with one hand, and quickly grab just forward of the hind legs as you pick the lizard up. Keep the tail end close to your body, hooking it under your armpit to hold it. A tail lashing can leave you with severe abrasions. For a vicious animal, throw a towel over its head, and then grab it as directed above, anterior to the neck and hindquarters.

Once your monitor is used to you, handle it for short periods of time each day. This will go a long way toward keeping it tame as it grows up. A snappy and defensive baby monitor is no big deal, but a snappy and defensive adult monitor is a problem. Frequent handling will help you to avoid this problem.

Claw Manicure

Monitor toenails, like human fingernails, continue to grow throughout the lifetime of the lizard. The claws of varanids can be rapier sharp and clipping the claws back can be healthy for them. However claw trimming is a not a one-person affair. I found this out when I tried it on a 6-foot white-throated monitor (1.8 m) that would position itself on top of the enclosure in a relaxed posture. When I attempted to trim its rear toenails, its tail

The author with a large white-throated monitor. Only carry tame monitors in this fashion.

smacked me across the face and back of the head with a resounding slap! I did not attempt to do that again!

The best way to trim the claws—especially if this is your first time doing this—is to go to your veterinarian and ask him or her to trim the lizards' toenails while you hold it safely. Claw trimming requires two people—one to hold the lizard and the other to trim its nails. Never trim the nails too short. Only cut the tips of the toenails, so bleeding does not occur. Keep some styptic powder on hand to stop the bleeding, just in case you do cut the nail too short. When finished, return the lizard to its enclosure. Trimming toenails usually takes about 10 minutes.

Chapter 5

Feeding, Nutrition, and Growth

The adage "you are what you eat" definitely applies to monitors. If you feed them a poor diet, they will be unhealthy and stunted. Feed them a diet rich in nutrients and variety, and they will be robust and healthy. Proper feeding of any pet, monitors included, is critical to the well-being of that pet. As you'll see, there is more to feeding monitors than tossing a mouse in the cage a few times a week.

Monitor lizards come in four predominant categories regarding food: insectivore, carnivore, scavenger, and omnivore. Some monitor lizards are active foragers that search for food, while others are ambush predators (e.g., Komodo and crocodile monitors) that sit and wait for food to come to them. African monitors are daily active foragers.

Like most juvenile monitor lizards around the world, African savannah monitor lizards are predominantly insectivores when younger. But by their third birthday, their teeth change and so does their diet. For the savannah and eyed monitors, it changes to a more durophagus (hard-shelled prey) diet (Cisse, 1972; Bennett, 2000, 2003). The white-throated monitor has a more varied diet, seasonally feeding on giant African snails (*Achatina*) and on assorted invertebrates, birds, snakes (including venomous species), and basically eating anything it can swallow (Auerbach, 1987; Branch, 1991; Alberts, 1994; Phillips, 1995; Lemm, 1996, 1997, 1998).

Among vertebrates, studies in sexual dimorphism have shown that males are often larger than females. The male monitor has a larger head and abdominal circumference than its female counterpart. The female has a longer SVL than a male of the same proportions (Brana, 1996). As we have seen, some white-throated monitor males also have a big head, which is advantageous in prey selection. Males tend to feed on a greater variety of prey items than do their female counterparts; this allows for less competition among conspecifics in the wild (and possibly in captivity). Males are less picky in prey selection than females are. Female monitors tend to feed more on calcium-rich prey items, especially just prior to and during a gravid period. Males need to grow bigger faster. Females also need to grow fast, but with a more mineral-enriched diet. I am sure this is a more common phenomenon throughout the Varanidae than most realize.

In nature, white-throated monitors are active hunters, constantly on the prowl for prey.

Monitor Feeding Behavior

A monitor lizard feeds in three stages:

1. The lizard picks up or bites off a piece of the prey.
2. The prey is moved from the front part of the mouth to the rear part of the mouth, with the tongue playing an active part in moving the prey posterior within the mouth.
3. The prey is swallowed.

The bite force of monitor lizards is considerable. They do not always apply their power in biting between their upper jaws and lower mandibles, but can apply force between each separately. This difference in power-phase bite force enables the monitor to apply both shearing and crushing power to a prey item, using the front teeth for shearing and applying the posterior teeth for crushing (Sinclair, 1987).

Monitor lizards have the extraordinary ability, like snakes do, to devour prey items larger than would seem possible. If your head size is proportionately larger than your body size, you can ingest larger prey and gain more nutrition per meal than a conspecific with a smaller head. This big-mouthed theme is seen in many monitor lizards, but in Africa it is most notably seen in the white-throated monitor. "Big-headed" hatchlings turn into "big-mouthed" adults. These big-mouthed monitors can eat faster than smaller mouthed animals can—prey swallowed faster does not always die immediately (swallowed alive). I observed a 6.5-foot male white-throated monitor ingest eight 2-week old chicks amazingly quickly, and I could hear the chicks chirping inside the bloated white-throat for several minutes. When living with monitor lizards, one must be prepared for such scenarios, as unpleasant as this might seem.

Monitor Teeth

The first treatise on reptile teeth appeared in an amazing book, *Odontography* (1840-1845), published as a two-volume set by the great Victorian paleontologist Richard Owen. In Volume I (1840), Owen has marvelous illustrations of monitor lizard teeth. The teeth of an animal tell you a lot about how it lives and what it eats. Monitor lizards have continuous tooth replacement almost until old age, at which time they have to gum their food or die of starvation.

Monitors often have teeth with serrated edges. Older savannah monitors grow teeth that are more flattened for crushing hard-shelled prey.

Cannibalism

All monitor lizards cannibalize, as some unfortunate keepers have discovered where once there were three monitors in an enclosure and later only one robust one (Cisse, 1972; Rippy, pers. obs.). It is a good idea to keep your younger monitor lizards solitary. Adults of equal size can cohabitate, provided you offer them each ample basking, feeding, sleeping, and hide spots to reduce undue stress between them.

African monitor lizards have two sets of teeth during their lifetime, baby teeth and adult teeth. Their baby teeth are sharp and designed for shearing and puncturing prey and feeding on insects. Their adult teeth replace the pointy insectivorous teeth and are large, round peg-shaped molar-like teeth designed for crushing mollusks and assorted hard-shelled prey, snails, beetles, crickets, etc. They are known as durophagus teeth. All African monitors have this durophagus tooth design, which is an adaptation to their dietary needs. Some African monitors feed mostly on insects (savannah and eyed monitors), others on *Achatina* snails and vertebrates (white-throated and Yemen monitors, *Varanus yemenensis*), while still others feed on shellfish and crocodile eggs (Nile and forest Nile monitors).

What to Feed Your Monitor

There has been much debate whether or not rodents are a healthy food source for savannah monitor lizards in captivity. From some studies, rodents are clearly unnatural in their wild diets; rodents are nocturnal and monitor lizards are diurnal, so they rarely encounter one another (Cisse, 1972, Branch, 1991; Bennett, 2003). In captivity, I observed how unnatural the white-throated monitors appeared to be when offered rodents. They ripped them apart with their claws (eviscerating them), crushed them in their jaws, often spitting them out before ingesting them.

The majority of the prey that savannah, eyed, and white-throated monitors consume in the wild is invertebrates. While many pet stores still advise hobbyists to feed their monitors rodents, a varied diet of various invertebrates (insects, shellfish, etc.) and few rodents is a better regimen.

Insects

Crickets are the most easily obtainable of the feeder insects. They can be purchased at local pet shops. If you need large quantities or specific sizes (although even hatchling savannahs can usually eat adult crickets), your pet store will likely be able to order them for you. If not, there are many suppliers available online that will deliver boxes of crickets right to your door.

Mealworms are another common feeder insect. These are the larvae of various beetle species. The mealworm that is best for monitors is the king mealworm or the superworm. These are very large mealworms that are highly digestible.

There are a number of other feeder insects available, although they are not as common, and your local pet store may not carry them. You can find suppliers of these insects online, in classified sections of reptile publications, and at herp expos. A few good examples that you find are silkworms, tomato hornworms, locusts, various species of roaches, and stick insects. Stick insects are illegal to keep in some areas, so check local laws before purchasing them. Some of the roaches are very large and therefore are excellent to feed large savannah monitors. Silkworms get quite large and have a high calcium content.

Gut-Loading Gut-loading is the process of feeding your feeder insects nutritious food before you feed them to your apex predator—your pet monitor. When your monitor eats the gut-loaded insects, they will pass on the benefits of the nutritious food they have eaten. Crickets, mealworms, and roaches are easy to gut-load. Other insects may have a special diet; follow the feeding instructions of your supplier for those species.

It is fairly easy to gut-load your feeders. In some form of escape-proof container, place your feeders, some hiding areas (paper towel tubes work well), and the gut-loading food. You can buy commercial gut-load or make your own. To make your own, blend a few of the following items: wheat germ, unflavored baby cereal, alfalfa powder, whole grain flour, and tropical fish flakes. You can put this in a low bowl or jar lid, or you can just put it in the bottom of the container. For moisture

Silkworms make a great food for monitor lizards. They are generally available from online herp supply companies.

and some additional nutrition, add a few pieces of orange, squash, sweet potato, carrots, or the stems of leafy green vegetables. Allow the insects to feed for 24 hours before feeding to your monitor. With mealworms, you need to make the layer of food deep enough for them to bury themselves, and only put thin slices of the moisture source on top of the food. Clean your gut-loading container and replace uneaten fruits and vegetables as needed—the more often the better.

Other Invertebrates

African monitors relish all types of shellfish, such as shrimp, snails, and crayfish. Shellfish can be purchased at your local fish market, bait shop, and supermarket. Crayfish can be purchased locally if you live in the southern US. They are also sometimes sold in pet stores. Some also carry large pond snails. Large earthworms can be harvested from your own backyard, if you don't use pesticides or fertilizers. They can also be purchased at bait shops and some pet stores.

Rodents

Rodents are easy to buy at most pet stores that sell reptiles. You can buy them live or frozen. While most monitor keepers feed live mice and rats to their lizards, a frozen and thawed rodent will never bite and injure your pet. If you feed frozen rodents, make sure they are thawed to room temperature before feeding. Do not thaw them in the microwave.

Mice and rats are sold in various sizes. Pinkies are hairless newborns, suitable for juvenile monitors. Fuzzies are baby rodents that have just grown in their hair. Hoppers are baby rodents, and there are progressively larger sizes of adult mice and rats. When feeding rodents to your monitor, choose a size

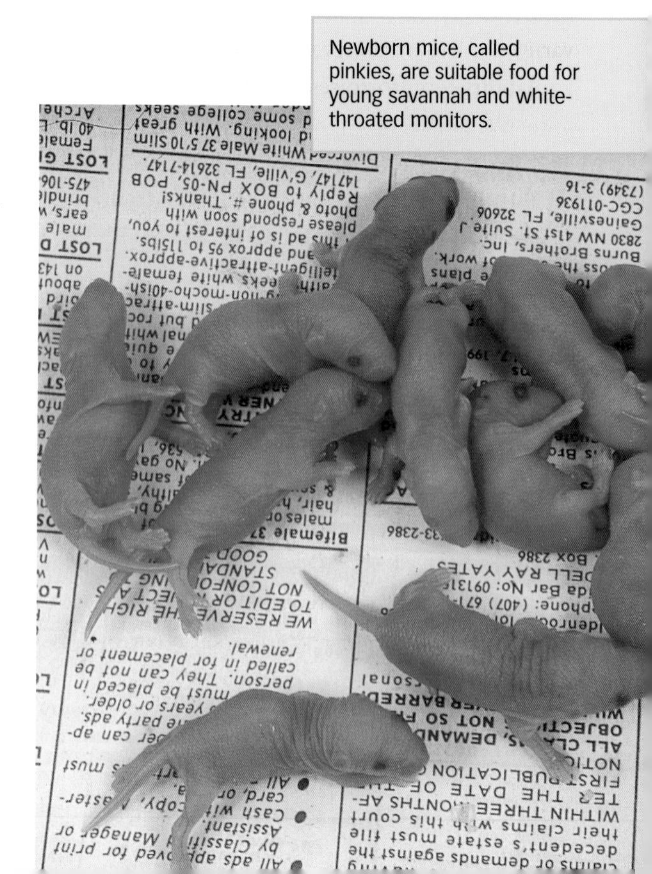

Newborn mice, called pinkies, are suitable food for young savannah and white-throated monitors.

that is not bigger than about half the size of the monitor's head.

You can also offer other vertebrate prey, including whole fish, baby chicks, and ground turkey. Boiled and cooled eggs make a good healthy treat.

Feeding the Savannah Monitor

Juvenile savannah monitors prey predominantly upon crickets (60 percent), slugs (18 percent), and assorted prey items; while adults prey predominantly on millipedes (50 percent), beetles (21 percent), and assorted other prey when made available (Cisse, 1972; Bayless, 1992; Bennett, 2000, 2003:20-22). Feed juvenile savannah monitors small meals every day, and adults larger meals three to four times a week. Vitamin enrichment (through gut-loading) should also be added to their live prey for balanced mineral levels. Clean water should be available to them at all times.

Feeding the White-Throated Monitor

Unlike the savannah monitor, adult white-throated monitor lizards prey on a greater variety of larger vertebrates. In the South African wild, they feed—according to availability—on tortoises, beetles, and grasshoppers, which make up a majority of their diet (Branch, 1991).

I have offered my African monitor lizards snails (European brown snails, *Helix aspersa*) and crayfish, which they seemed to enjoy and even recognized as prey. They swallowed the smaller snails whole; they cracked the larger ones' shells, spit the snail out or shook the snail from the shell, and then swallowed their escargot meal.

If you offer your monitors crayfish, wash them off in cold water first. They can be purchased at bait shops, fish markets, online suppliers, and sometimes pet stores. The white-

Adult rats can only be fed to very large monitors, such as adult white-throats.

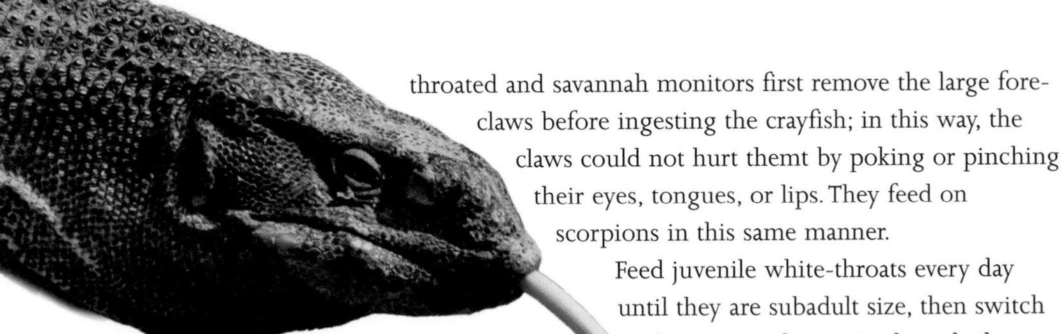

Even large white-throated monitors prey largely on invertebrates—not rodents—in the wild.

throated and savannah monitors first remove the large fore-claws before ingesting the crayfish; in this way, the claws could not hurt themt by poking or pinching their eyes, tongues, or lips. They feed on scorpions in this same manner.

Feed juvenile white-throats every day until they are subadult size, then switch them to moderate sized meals three to four times per week.

Feeding the Eyed Monitor

The eyed monitor's natural diet is similar to that of the savannah monitor. Eyed monitors that I have had paid no attention to rodents when they were offered, preferring invertebrate prey, especially centipedes (*Lulus spp.*), which they attacked and fed upon with fervor. Feed juveniles small meals daily, and moderate- to large-sized meals of insects to adults every other day.

Herbivory and Monitor Lizards

Some monitor lizards, such as the green tree monitor (*Varanus prasinus*), Asian water monitor (*Varanus salvator*), savannah monitor (*Varanus exanthematicus*), white-throated monitor (*Varanus albigularis*), and Nile monitor (*Varanus niloticus*), have been offered fruit, which they readily accepted (Balsai, 1997b). Could these monitor lizards be considered omnivorous (feeding on both plant and animal matter)? There are two Philippine monitor lizards, the Gray's monitor (*Varanus olivaceus*) and the Panay monitor (*Varanus mabitang*), that are partial or obligate herbivores (part-time or exclusive plant eaters).

There are a few reports of savannah monitors feeding on ripe bananas (Cisse, 1972; Keshner, pers. com.). Why would these primary insectivores feed on fruit? Bananas are a rich source of potassium and calcium, and more importantly, of water. Bananas possess calcium, niacin, iron, and phosphorus—vital minerals required, especially during oogenesis, or egg production. The author and fellow keepers noted their white-throated monitors fed on strawberries; even when offered other food items, the lizards selected the fruit. Following the big mess they made feeding on the fruit, they did appear to enjoy them.

Was it the color that attracted them? I have observed my savannah monitors feed regularly on red rose petals in my garden, ignoring the yellow or pink flowers. Could the color of the plant material trigger a feeding response? To date, little is known of this herbivorous behavior among the Varanidae, but these are not isolated cases (Balsai, 1997b).

Inappropriate Foods

A hungry monitor lizard will eat what is available to it, so it is up to the keeper of animals in captivity to make sure their diet is nutritionally balanced and appropriate for the particular species. Feeding inappropriate foods to your monitor with little enrichment and variety will lead to illness and death. Variety in the food offered is the key to your monitor lizard's health and longevity. How does one evaluate a monitor lizard's health? Observe its behavior. Is it active, bright eyed, climbing, walking, running, digging, basking, and sleeping? If it is behaving normally, then your lizard is probably doing fine.

There are a number of inappropriate items that are often recommended as monitor food. Dog food contains a high fat-to-protein ratio, higher than that of the natural prey of African monitors. Much of the protein in dog food is wheat, soybean, and rice products. Monitor lizards were designed to ingest animal

Dog food should not be offered to monitors as it is high in fat.

Making a Monitor Menu

If you are unsure what to feed your monitor lizard, here is a simple test to see what it prefers to feed on: Place a number of different types of food items on paper plates, each type on its own plate. Watch and see which items the lizard chooses. Try this many times and you will quickly see which prey items your lizard prefers. The monitor knows what it needs more than you do, and it is the keeper's job to facilitate the lizard's nutritional welfare as best he can. It may eat all of the contents on all of the plates, but note which food items it eats first, second, third, etc.

protein, not vegetables and not such a high fat content. Feeding dog food regularly will result in an obese monitor that probably will suffer liver problems. Chicken parts and giblets are also not a balanced diet and may promote the growth of *Salmonella* bacteria. Any meat or prey items that have been frozen for more than three months will have lost a significant amount of vitamins and minerals. Avoid feeding canned monitor or tegu food of any kind to your monitor lizard, as they have not been on the market long enough to be sure they are good for your lizard. Last, I will again stress that feeding a rodent-only diet will lead to obesity, other health problems, and boredom.

Nutrition

Variety is the key to a monitor lizard's nutritional needs. What one prey item does not offer in the way of protein, carbohydrates, minerals, and vitamins can be supplemented by other prey items, giving the monitor an overall balanced diet as well as variety.

It is always advisable to learn what the animal eats in the wild and duplicate that diet in captivity. Feed the animal what it prefers to eat.

Supplements

Vitamin deficiency is a primary source of malnutrition and illness in monitor lizards today. When your monitor is offered whole-body foods (such as rodents), there are usually sufficient vitamins and minerals within the food to avoid adding additional supplements. You may wish to consider this when your animals come out of their inactive hibernation periods and when the females are feeding heavily in preparation for production of eggs. At these times, supplementation of vitamins and minerals may be a good idea.

Breeding female monitors require more vitamin and mineral supplements than nonbreeding animals.

You can add items like calcium and multivitamins to their meals by sprinkling them onto insects in a "shake and bake" technique: place insects and calcium/vitamin powder into a bag and gently shake it until the insects are coated with the powder. Feed the prey to the monitors immediately, so that no significant amounts of the supplements fall off. Do not overdo it with the supplements. Juveniles and breeding females only need supplementation once or twice a week. Nonbreeding adults should not be given supplements more than twice a month normally, and perhaps once a week for the first month after coming out of hibernation or aestivation.

Choose a vitamin/mineral supplement designed for reptiles or a high-quality human supplement. If using a human supplement, you will need to use a coffee grinder or something similar to pulverize the tablets. Check the expiration dates and dispose of expired supplements.

Calcium

Calcium is a vital mineral required by all animal and plant life for proper metabolic processes. Because young vertebrates grow very fast, they require high levels of dietary calcium. Insufficient dietary calcium can cause metabolic bone disease (MBD), which is "soft bone" malady. Younger lizards should be given daily calcium supplements with each insect meal. This may seem labor intensive, but is very important at this stage of development.

Calcium sources can be had inexpensively. You can purchase calcium powder at your local market. Multiple vitamins can also be offered, but do not have sufficient levels of calcium, so mix your calcium and multiple vitamin powders together. Younger animals and breeding female monitors require more calcium than adults and nonbreeding animals.

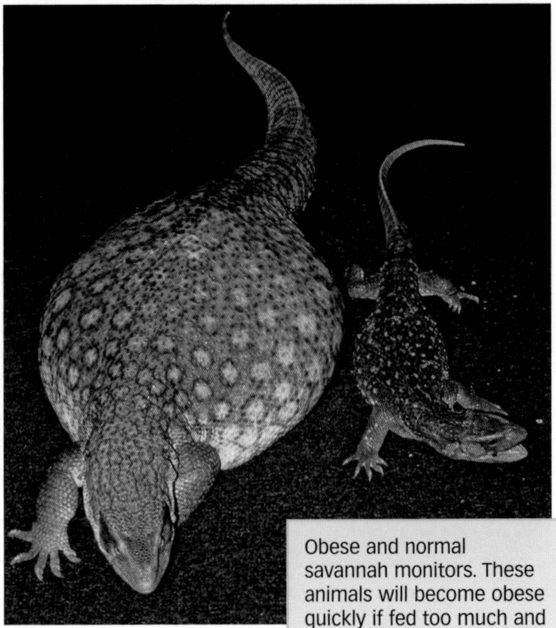

Obese and normal savannah monitors. These animals will become obese quickly if fed too much and exercised too little.

How to Feed Your Monitor

As hunters, monitor lizards should be encouraged to forage for food, and that suggests activity patterns conducive to this. Some of these activities could include feeding live prey so they can run down their food, including tree branches in the enclosure so they can look for insect prey above the ground, and a using deep substrate so they can dig for hidden prey. Make monitors work for their food. In this way, you reduce the proclivities for a sedentary and obese monitor lizard and allow it to exhibit more natural behaviors.

The African monitor lizards have home ranges and patrol their territories seeking out every nook, cranny, tree, and hole for an edible morsel. In captivity, you should place live prey items (i.e., insects, pinky mice, wax worms, etc.) into your lizard's terrarium when it is not aware of it and let it find the food. This both stimulates your monitor's mental capacities and provides it with needed exercise.

When not offering live prey, such as whole fish, prekilled rats, and such, I always serve it on a large white paper plate to signal to the monitor lizards that food was served on white-paper plates and not from my white hands; this is known as conditioning. When offered live prey, the same pair of medical hemostats was used during every feeding event. In this way, the monitor learned very quickly that hands should not be mistaken with food. Try to feed your monitor lizards at the same time on the same days, establishing a routine both parties can live with.

Monitor lizards learn to associate certain colors with food. If you feed your monitor lizard a lot of rats, then your monitor will soon learn to associate all things white with food. They can even associate the rattling sound inside a brown paper bag with rodents, so be aware that when you enter a room with their food in a paper bag, your monitor lizard most likely will already know it's feeding time.

Feed your monitor as much food as it will eat in about 15 minutes. It is best to feed earlier in the day rather than later. This allows it to digest while the cage is warm, instead of eating at the end of the day and becoming too cool at night to digest food. Hatchling and juvenile savannah, eyed, and white-throated monitors should be fed daily. Adults need only be fed three to four times a week.

Obesity

Wild monitor lizards are active all day long and their food sources are often scant, thus, their metabolism and constitution have evolved such that these lizards may survive on small rations. In captivity, however, a great many monitors will exist under the exact opposite conditions—too much to eat and too little activity. The result is an obese and unhealthy reptilian lump. Signs of obesity include listlessness, sluggishness, slow movements, labored breathing, and a generally fat appearance. Obesity leads to myriad health problems and even death from heart failure. Combat obesity by feeding smaller or less frequent meals, feeding more insects and other invertebrates rather than rodents, and giving your monitor opportunities to exercise.

Diet Cycles

Unlike many other monitor lizards, African species hibernate during the colder months and aestivate during the warmer months, naturally going off feed on a seasonal basis. During these inactivity periods, they stay in a burrow, up in a tree, or in a termite mound for several months, remaining inactive for a majority of that time.

Your captive husbandry should reflect this pattern. You will notice your animals engage in their African cycles, becoming inactive and listless and ceasing much of their daily activities. This will occur roughly from November to February for both savannah and white-throated monitors, and again during April for white-throats. During the warmer months (November to February), temperatures can be hot (about 100°F/37.8°C) The animals will tell you when these physiological conditions are occurring by their behavior: decreased activity and less feeding (Cisse, 1972; Phillips, 1995; Dieter, 1997; Lemm, 1998).

If you house your monitors together, be careful when feeding them. They may fight over a food item and could get injured.

During their off-feed times, their dietary intake will decrease as compared to their active season. It is important when the animals are in their active mode to feed them all they will eat in a 15–20 minute period, with ambient temperatures high (about 100°F/37.8°C). All African monitor lizards do this (including desert monitors *Varanus griseus*), unlike other monitor lizards elsewhere that do not do this on a annual basis. Observe the animals and watch where they spend their time in regard to temperature and adjust them accordingly. Captive-bred and long-term captive African monitors display these same behaviors, as evidenced by the reproduction behavior detailed in Chapter 6.

Growth and Size

Growth rates are directly related to diet, temperature, and competition. If the diet is lacking in proper nutrients, minerals, or vitamins, the lizard may become malnourished, even though it is eating. When you feed a balanced diet, induce the animal to exercise, and provide it with sufficient heat and clean water, the likelihood of a healthy captive life greatly increases. Monitors that are offered a natural variety of prey items grow faster than those animals offered only mice!

Lizards offered a high-protein diet, such as rodents or dog food, grow incredibly fast within the first year of life. Such animals are often easily recognizable because their heads are proportionately smaller than their bodies, giving them a pinhead (microcephalic) appearance. Animals fed exclusively on rodents, dog food, and/or cat food may have metabolic problems later, such as liver dysfunction, renal failure, or cardiac problems. Feeding African monitors these high-protein foods in a high-heat environment constrains them from metabolizing food and energy; reptiles cannot maintain this level of metabolic and gastronomic activity for very long and often die without warning. Hence, many African monitors fed on such a diet die young. Canned pet food is not recommended for these animals.

A healthy subadult savannah monitor has an average growth rate of three-quarters of an inch (1.9 cm) per month. A 9-inch (22.9 cm) hatchling can grow to about 54 inches (137.2 cm) in four years (Madden, pers. com.). One hatchling savannah monitor was 6-inches (15.2 cm) long when purchased and grew to 54 inches (137.2 cm) in total length in 5.5 years (Henderson, pers. obs.).

No Hand-Feeding!

Do not hand-feed your monitor. Use tongs, hemostats, a paper bag, a paper plate, etc. to offer your monitor lizards their food. In this way, your hands are less likely to become part of the meal you are offering. Also, it prevents your monitor from forming an association between food and your hands. Never take your monitor lizard for granted. Know that it can, if it is so motivated, inflict injuries upon your person, especially if you are careless.

The white-throated monitor is a much hardier and gluttonous feeder and grows at a faster rate than the savannah monitor, perhaps as much as 1-1.5 inches (2.5-3.8 cm) and as much as 1.5 pounds (0.5 kg) per month (Baker, pers. com.). Gogga Brown (1834-1920) received three white-throat hatchlings that he fed natural foods, and they grew one-quarter of an inch (5.6mm) per day (Branch, 1991:92)! Gerard Visser, Curator of Reptiles at the Rotterdam Zoo (Netherlands) reported his hatchlings grew 10 times their hatchling weight in 6 months (Branch, 1991:92; G. Visser, pers. com.).

The eyed monitor is predominantly an insectivore, so a great deal of insects should be offered to them. Their growth rates are unknown, but are probably comparable to that of the savannah monitor.

Shedding

The faster a lizard grows, the more often it sheds its skin. Older animals shed less frequently than younger animals do because they grow at a much slower rate. Shedding

When well-cared for, baby savannah and white-throated monitors grow at a tremendous rate for the first year or two.

usually begins at the pelvic region, with the head and tail ends free of shed skin first. Gogga Brown noted adults finished a shed within 35 days, whereas a juvenile could go through two sheds within the same period of time (Branch, 1991:97).

Age and Longevity

Monitor lizards grow fast and keep growing until death. The older these lizards get, the slower their growth rates are, especially after sexual maturity, when growth rates slow down dramatically. Dr. Greg Erickson of Florida State University, Tallahassee, has discovered that, like the rings of a tree, growth rates can be measured by counting the concentric annual rings in the dermal ossicles, or bone that resides under each of the monitor lizard's scales. These dermal ossicles have shown that monitor lizards that maintain a juvenile growth rate for a longer period of time prior to sexual maturity can attain monstrous proportions (Erickson et al., 2003).

Pet animals often have a longer life span than their wild counterparts do; I kept a savannah monitor for 14.5 years. The longevity record for the white-throated monitor is 6095 days, or 16.6 years for an individual that was approximately 3-4 years old when captured (Branch, 1991:82). The older a white-throated monitor gets, the more prominent and bulbous its nose becomes. As a monitor lizard approaches its geriatric age (about 15-20 years), its teeth fall out

If provided with a proper environment and fresh, varied foods, most captive monitor lizards can live 20 years or more in captivity, with their wild counterparts living 10 or more years (Buffrenil and Naclerio, pers. com.).

Water

Water is life. Without water, all life perishes. When introducing a new monitor lizard to its enclosure, show it the water container. Bring your new lizard to the water basin and allow it to drink. Many baby lizards have died because they did not know where the water dish was. The container should be low to the ground or buried into the substrate for easy access, and it should not be too deep (especially for hatchlings). If it is deep, place a stone in the water dish, so crickets and young monitors can climb on it and not drown.

Clean water should be provided daily. Make sure the basin is sturdy and not easily flipped over. If it is flimsy, your lizard will be flipping the water basin over every day, and this can result in a muddy, moldy substrate, a dirty animal, and unnecessary cleaning time for you.

Water is especially critical when a high-protein diet, such as rodents, is offered. The nitrogenous waste from protein catabolism (digestion) in birds and reptiles is uric acid. The production of high concentrations of uric acid enhances water conservation in the reptile and produces an internal precipitate that can permeate organ surfaces, a condition known as hyperuricemia. Hyperuricemia can lead to organ failure and death. So water becomes a critical diluting agent when high-protein prey items are fed to monitors. Also, if water intake is insufficient, uric acid levels will rise, and along with ingested rodent hair cause dehydration. When this happens, the urea and rodent hair will harden into a hair mass that will have to be surgically removed or can cause intestinal impaction, which often results in the death of younger monitors.

Not Too Much

I must offer a word of caution about overfeeding. Hobbyists must not be overly enthusiastic about feeding their pets, lest they grow obese. The three monitors discussed in this book are all prone to becoming obese in captivity. Establishing and adhering to a proper feeding schedule is paramount in ensuring the long-term health of our dragons.

Pet white-throated monitors can live for 17 years or more.

Chapter 6

Breeding

Once you have kept monitors for a while and have a thorough grasp of their husbandry, you may want to try breeding them. Breeding any of the monitors, the African monitors included, is not commonplace in the herp hobby. It requires a lot of space and time. However, because the African monitors in the wild are under pressure from human development, wild collecting of these lizards may be prohibited. At that time, captive breeding will be the only source of African monitors for the hobby.

In nature, white-throated monitors are seasonal breeders, mating in the early summer. They usually retain this pattern in captivity.

Another reason why the African monitors are not bred frequently is the lack of financial return. Because they are imported in large numbers very cheaply, the price of savannah monitors is fairly low. Breeding this species in captivity will probably cost more than the breeder can expect to earn back. White-throated monitors usually command higher prices, and consequently they are more frequently bred than their cousins. This is not to suggest that money is the only reason to breed a reptile, but it certainly is a consideration.

Seasonality

Some herptoculturalists say that when reptiles are moved from one hemisphere to another (e.g., Africa to California), they shift their breeding cycles to the seasons of that hemisphere after approximately three years. This is not so with African monitor lizards. Like feeding, reproduction is a seasonal affair for these lizards; breeding is determined by the season. Seasonal cycles of reproduction are characteristic of reptiles from temperate regions, whereby the reproduction of tropical forms is frequently acyclic or continuous (Cloudsley-Thompson 1999:171-172). Hence, subtropical reptiles (African monitor lizards) are stimulated to breed by the temperature increase that they experience when they emerge from aestivation and not necessarily from hibernation.

African monitors mate during the hot summer months, and then go dormant for the remainder of the summer (from September to February), not eating, mating, or doing much of anything but aestivating. The white-throated monitor is least active from April to July (Cisse, 1976; Branch, 1991:102). African monitors may pop out of their burrows or trees on a warm day but will return to their retreats by nightfall. They do not eat much during these summer months. They fast, using their stored fat reserves for nourishment.

Female monitors require more calcium than males do, especially during the reproductive period when they require high levels of it to properly produce eggs. If the female does not attain sufficient dietary calcium, she will take it from her own femur/leg bones and metabolize it for egg production (Buffrenil, 2001). Some animals remove so much calcium from their legs that they lose the ability to walk! If the female cannot attain sufficient calcium levels, she will not breed that season and can succumb to metabolic deficiencies that may leave her extremely weak, or even kill her. The dietary preference of males versus females indicates that there is sexual dimorphism in their dietary uptake, especially during the August/September and March/April months.

Sexing African Monitors

The reproductive structures of monitors are all internal, unlike those of mammals. Male lizards and snakes have paired copulatory organs, called hemipenes (singular: hemipenis). When the male monitor is sexually excited, his hemipenes fill with blood and evert out of the cloaca. A male may use either or both of his hemipenes to mate with a female. Monitor lizards seem to instantly know each other's gender,

Adult male savannah monitors sometimes will evert their hemipenes (circled in red) when they defecate.

which is suggestive of the presence of pheromones or other signaling chemicals.

It is not easy to sex a monitor lizard. Probing them, a technique often used to sex snakes, is ineffective. "Popping" a monitor lizard may work. This technique involves pressing the base of the tail with your thumb in order to get the hemipenes to evert or pop out. For immature animals, this technique is often harmful because you can crush the base of the tail and cause serious injury. It can also cause the monitor to defecate, vomit, and bite. In older monitors, it is difficult to cause the hemipenes to evert because the muscles of the cloaca are much stronger. Because of the chance of injuring your monitor, popping is not recommended.

Varanids exhibit sexual dimorphism in mature animals. Males have a wider head than females of equal age. The overall length of a male is roughly composed of half body and half tail. In the female, the head and body may be 60 percent of her length. It is theorized that females need the extra body length and girth to hold eggs (Visser, 1981:87; Brana, 1996). Male monitors have larger forelegs than females do.

The bulge on the lateral and ventral sides of a monitor's tail base may also tell you the sex of a monitor. Males have larger ventral tail base bulges than females do, but be aware that the tail is also used for fat storage. A fatter tail is going to push the hemi-structures

Cloned Monitors?

In 2005, it was discovered that monitor lizards may exhibit a reproductive strategy called parthenogenesis. In this form of reproduction, females reproduce without males, essentially creating clones of themselves in their eggs. Parthenogenesis is seen in several other types of lizards, notably geckos and whiptails (*Cnemidophorus*).

In most cases, varanids are usually bisexual, meaning that both a male and female parent are required to produce young. However, at least some species exhibit facultative parthenogenesis, meaning the female mother is able to switch from the normal bisexual mode of reproduction to unisexual parthenogenesis. This allows solitary females to reproduce when males are unavailable. Obviously, more research on the phenomenon is needed to elucidate the details.

Appreciation is extended to Bernd Eidenmueller for sharing information with the author on this account.

outward, so consider the time of year (hibernation, aestivation, gluttony months—all of which affect the fat in the tail base) and the head/body size of the animal when attempting to determine the sex of your animal. With practice, you can discern male from female animals just by looking at them.

Maturity

Female savannah monitors are sexually mature at approximately 26 inches (66.0 cm), with males mature at 28 inches (66-71 cm) total length (Rowell, pers. com.). Both size and age appear to be determining factors of a monitor lizard's sexual maturity. Prior to courtship behavior, white-throated monitors offer visual cues that can also help you determine when these animals are ready to breed. Male white-throated monitors change colors. The body turns reddish-brown, with a duller color on the neck ventral and banding turning a bright yellowish color. The lower jaws turn a light blue or purple hue. The female's body turns a browner color, with an enhanced black throat, and the scales between the eye and ear opening turning brick red.

Pair of savannah monitors engaged in courtship behavior. The male chases the female and flicks her with his tongue.

Courtship Behavior

Courtship behavior among African monitors is a five-step affair that often takes place over several days. The act begins with the male pursuing the female. The male will chase the female and mount her, moving its head rapidly from side to side, its tongue flicking her profusely. If the female is receptive, she will stop running and lift her tail, allowing the male to penetrate her. If she is resistant, she will run; but in captivity, she has nowhere to go so she will lay her body and tail flat to the ground. Courtship behavior can last a few hours or many days; it is most exhausting for the nonreceptive female and frustrating for the male.

Receptive females remain quiet, with the males ensuing with jerky head motions and tongue flicks. He will be seen attempting to lift her tail with his rear legs, moving the posterior end of his body to her flanks, with his cloaca as close to her cloaca as possible. They may appear awkward and almost clumsy. Once the female lifts her tail and allows copulation, they may remain in this position for some time. To further his contact with the female, the male may wrap his tail around hers.

Once they have mated, the pair separate, but may resume copulation later; the males are in rut and can think of little else to do during this period. Once the female has been fertilized, she will not accept any other

If the female is receptive, courtship progresses to mating.

White-throated monitors mating. This is the most commonly bred of the African monitors.

male's advances and will avoid them. These females will attempt to escape further copulations, keeping their bellies and tails flat to the ground thereafter.

Ritualized Combat

Ritualized combat is very similar to other combat behaviors, but it is not viscious. Among males and females, this is a mixed affair; the males wrestle with the females, and the females wrestle with the males (Horn et al., 1994; Wesiak, 1998). Victorious males and their opposing female counterparts also combat. First the male combats with the female, then the female combats with the male, and then reproduction ensues (Wesiak, 1998). This "dance" involves circling, mounting, head jerking, nape scratching, tripoding (standing on hind legs and tail) and wrestling, whereby the victor pushes the other down, pursues them, and mates with them (Horn et al., 1994). I have never seen a savannah monitor wrestle or clinch-phase, but I have seen them tripod, so they are probably capable of wrestling (Bayless, 1994; Attum et al., 2000).

Within home ranges when they are in estrus, females combat for rights to mate with dominant males. It has been suggested that once a female monitor has observed male/male combat and has engaged in female/male combat, she chooses her mate and engages in courtship behavior.

Double Clutching ...or Not?

Some breeding events suggest these animals are able to double-clutch, that is, to deposit more than a single clutch during their breeding seasons (Pierson, pers. obs.). Captive observations are suggestive that they may be able to do this in the wild. Of course sufficient food and resources would be required for them to accomplish this successfully.

Gestation

If the mating is successful and both parties are fertile, eggs will start to develop. When a female reptile is gestating, she is said to be *gravid* rather than pregnant. Following mating, the female will keep the eggs within her body cavity while they develop for four to eight weeks before depositing them into a nest hole. During this time, she may feed more at first and then less so as she gains bulk and approaches egg laying. She may drink more and feed on smaller sized prey items. One keeper observed his female white-throat vomit only mucus several times during her gestation period; perhaps he was observing his monitor exhibit morning sickness (R. Williams, pers. obs.)!

Some keepers recommend separating the male from the female after fertilization has occurred, but others suggest keeping them together. I recommend separating the male from the female about three weeks after their mating event, or when she begins to bulk up and appear like a lumpy pillowcase. During this period, she can be aggressive toward her cagemates and you, so beware. Keeping her isolated will reduce her stress levels about egg predation. Gestationusually takes from three to eight weeks between the time she has copulated to when she digs her burrow to deposit her eggs.

Nesting

With increased abdominal size and nocturnal behavior, your female is probably seeking proper sites in the enclosure to dig a nest (Irwin et al., 1996). When it is time for your animal to deposit her eggs, she will dig profusely, sticking her nose and tongue into the substrate, tongue flicking and searching for an appropriate place with the proper soil temperature. She excavates the burrow using her claws to move the earth. She digs like a dog does, using the forelegs for excavating and the rear legs for moving the earth behind her. I have always wondered why African monitors have a table-top flat head and found out when observing video taken of my animals—when the female was digging soil from the

The abdomens of gravid monitors greatly enlarge over the course of gestation.

ceiling of the burrow, she used the occipital part of her head (above the eyes) as a trowel, carving the burrow out using her head like a steam shovel.

To deposit her eggs, savannah monitors may dig a shallow hole, perhaps 10 inches (25.4 cm) deep, or deeper depending on the substrate and ambient temperature. When a female white-throat has found a proper nesting area, she will dig a burrow approximately 6 to 10 inches (15-25 cm) deep and then cover it up neatly. If she cannot find a suitable place to bury her eggs, she will deposit them here and there.

The female will continue to dig her burrow until it meets her requirements of proper soil content, temperature, and humidity. She may dig for a few hours or even several days time, taking intermittent rest periods when required. Although the ambient and ground temperatures in Africa may fluctuate and are often very high during this hot season, the temperature of the soil 6-10 inches (15-25 cm) below the surface remains fairly constant and conducive to egg incubation proclivities.

Following egg deposition, she will bury the eggs and protect them—be careful, as the female can be extremely aggressive at this time (Adragna, Williams, pers. obs.). Several keepers (Brown, Faust, Williams, pers. obs.) have seen white-throated monitors deposit their eggs in one place and move them to another safer site for burial and incubation.

The eggs of monitor lizards are not hard like chicken eggs, but somewhat leathery and even pliable when first deposited. These eggs are a demonstration of the delicate and intricate works of nature: they let enough moisture in, but not enough to drown them, and they let sufficient carbon dioxide out. Proper temperature, humidity, and substrate determine these aforementioned factors.

For a makeshift burrow, use a wastepaper basket with a round hole cut out in the side and fill it with a mixture of peat, potting soil, and oak leaves partially buried into the substrate. It will appear most inviting to your females as an egg laying depository (Williams, pers. obs.). If she likes this nest, she will deposit her eggs in it; if she does not, she will excavate elsewhere in the terrarium. If she cannot find a proper nest site, she may simply deposit her eggs in the open, in the water, etc. Once she has found a suitable place, she will deposit her eggs, often doing so at night.

Artificial incubators can be procured and even constructed from several sources. Check your local reptile-oriented pet shop, the Internet at www.Varanus/forums, and your local herpetological society for further details on this. In some lizards, the sex of the hatchlings is determined by the incubation temperatures. However, this does not seem to be the case with

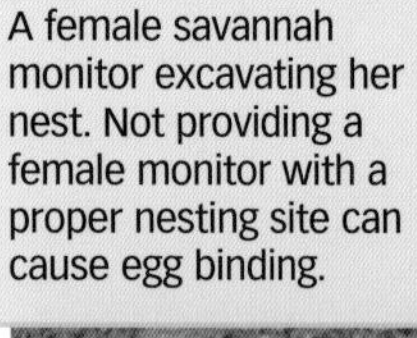

A female savannah monitor excavating her nest. Not providing a female monitor with a proper nesting site can cause egg binding.

African monitors. They have male and female sex chromosomes, just like mammals.

The largest clutch for any savannah monitor was 54 eggs by a single white-throated monitor (Faust, pers. com.), but specific data for this event is sadly lacking. Large clutches of eggs have been noted by groups of monitors living together, which makes it difficult to determine which females deposited which eggs (Duinen, 1983; Bayless, 1994; MacInnes, St. Pierre, pers. obs.). The average clutch size depends on the size of the female, but from most information on reproduction behavior of *Varanus exanthematicus* and *Varanus albigularis*, you can expect approximately 12 eggs for *V. exanthematicus* and 25 eggs for *V. albigularis*.

Eggs Without Mating?

Female monitors will sometimes produce eggs, even without the presence of a male. Nobody is quite clear about why this occurs, but the end result is that the female will lay a large number of infertile eggs. The female still puts a lot of resources into the eggs (the yolk, in particular, is full of nutrients, and the shells require calcium), so it is still a good idea to add additional calcium and nutrients to her diet during this period. Also, provide her with a nesting spot, so she does not retain the eggs and become egg bound.

White-throated monitor eggs incubating in moist vermiculite.

Problems With Egg Laying

Female monitors will occasionally have problems laying their eggs, a condition known as dystocia or egg binding. Essentially, the eggs are retained within the female's oviduct, where they can cause serious problems if they break down and rot, leading to infection and even death. If your female does not return to her normal behavior several weeks after her eggs should have been laid or reabsorbed, check with your local vet to be sure she is not retaining eggs.

Multi-Clutching

In the wild, after the female has deposited her clutch, she may have used over 50 percent of her energy to do so, and she is unable to deposit more eggs. However, in captivity food sources are plentiful and levels of calcium are higher, so she may be able to deposit a second clutch of eggs within 60 days of the first clutch. This is called multi-clutching. As with the first clutch, the female tastes the soil with her tongue, sticks her nose into it to smell it and, using her senses, will deposit her eggs again. In captivity, nesting resources are at a premium. With little choice of where she can lay her eggs, she might do so where she had deposited an earlier clutch (Pierson, Williams, pers. obs.).

Multi-clutching has not been seen in the wild populations of any monitor lizard species. We will define multi-clutching as two or more clutches deposited within a single breeding season. For an African monitor lizard, that would be from September through April. Multi-clutching has been observed among captive savannah monitor lizards (Brown, Branch, 1991; Pierson, Williams, pers. com.). When an African monitor deposits her eggs, it is usually at the beginning of the rainy or wet seasons, so that the eggs will hatch at the end of the rainy season. It seems that multi-clutching is related to food intake, calcium levels, ovum sizes, and perhaps courtship duration, sperm retention, and other unknown factors.

Hatchling savannah monitors are quite small and must be handled carefully.

Hatchlings

Hatchling monitor lizards are simply adorable—spitting images of their parents, ready to feed, fight, and sleep in typical reptile fashion. The health of the female parent determines the health of her eggs, and consequently her offspring, and much of this depends upon on calcium/mineral dietary uptake. Savannah monitors hatch from their nests from May to July, having incubated throughout the six-month dry season in Africa. When they emerge, the hot harmattan winds have passed and the locust swarms that prevail across West Africa begin, providing them with a seasonally abundant food resource.

Monitor hatchlings grow quickly (Bennett, 2003:24-26). They may be kept together until antagonistic behavior is observed, but they should then be separated to reduce stress levels. Do not place hatchlings with their parents, as they could become a snack for the larger lizards!

Overfeeding in hatchlings causes impaction, which can kill a young monitor very quickly. Be sure the babies have plenty of water, adequate temperature gradient, several hide spots, and items to climb to keep their muscles strong.

Post-Gravid Advice

Following her egg laying duties, your mother monitor will be exhausted, and having not eaten for several weeks, she will be cranky and hungry. Feed her as much as she will eat as soon as possible following egg deposition. Over half of her energy is used in egg deposition, and this same energy needs to be immediately replaced.

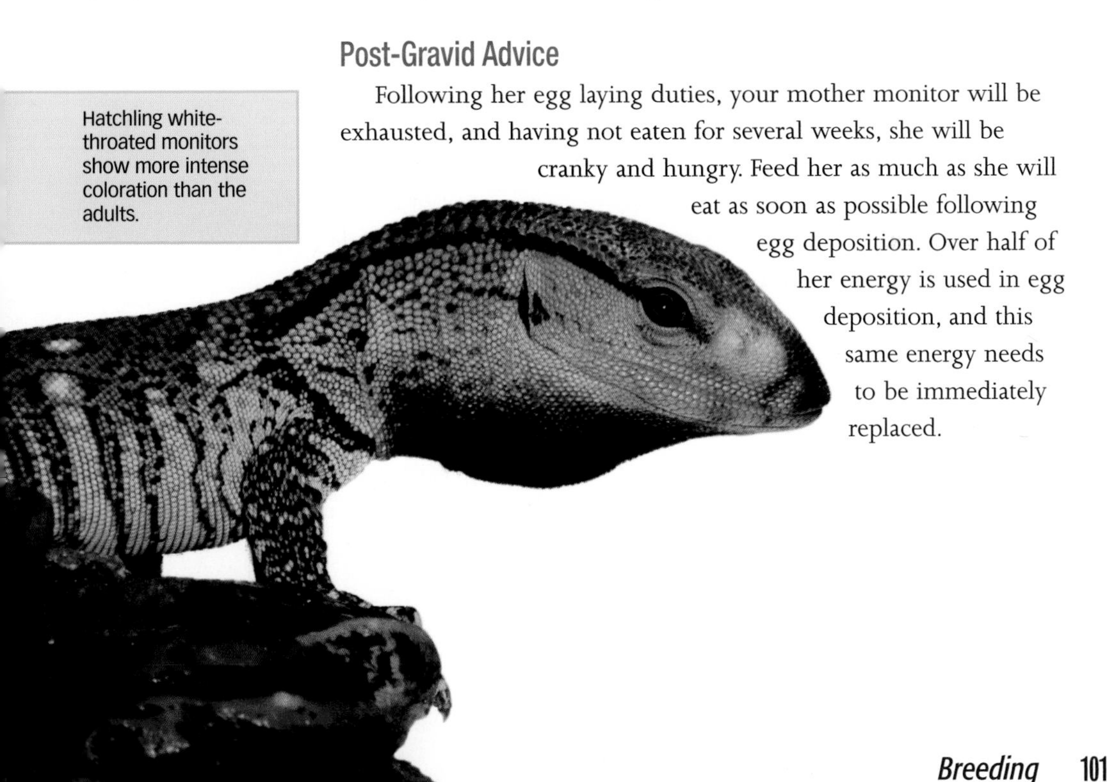

Hatchling white-throated monitors show more intense coloration than the adults.

Chapter 7

Health Care

Savannah monitors and their close relatives are hardy lizards that don't seem to come down with as many health problems as some other commonly kept reptiles do. As long as it is properly kept, a savannah monitor can live a long life as a pet. Most common health problems are the result of inadequate care.

South African archaeologist, naturalist, and paleontologist Alfred "Gogga" Brown (1834-1920) lived with 229 leguaans (*Varanus albigularis*) from 1868 to 1914. In captivity, he took comprehensive notes, recording every aspect of the monitor lizards lives. He reported how they died as well: severe falls (from trees); cold; pneumonia/pulmonary illness; ulcers, cysts, and tumors of the liver, ovary, viscera, and legs; enlargement of the liver, heart, bile duct, and stomach; cirrhosis; impaction; prolapsed bowel; egg bound; pinworms; paralysis; convulsions; poison (sheep dip); calcium deficiency (soft bones); and old age (Branch, 1991).

It is best to establish a relationship with a reptile veterinarian before you have an emergency.

Finding a Veterinarian

You should try to find a veterinarian who is knowledgeable about reptile medicine as soon as possible after you obtain your monitor. Taking your new pet to the vet for an initial visit can ward off problems down the road. If you don't have a vet, you can check with your local herpetological society or ask local pet shops if they can recommend someone that has experience with reptiles. If you cannot find help with those resources, go on the Internet and research the Association of Reptile and Amphibian Veterinarians at www.arav.com or other reptile/monitor lizard-oriented web pages or forums. It is best to use a vet educated in reptile medicine, but this is not always possible. If you can't find a reptile veterinarian, one who works with exotic animals is your next best choice.

Diet and Obesity

Obesity is a frequent cause of death among captive reptiles and is the result of too little exercise and an improper diet. It occurs when the body takes in more calories than it can use, hence it stores fat in body. As in humans and other animals, obesity puts tremendous strain on the heart and liver, along with the muscles and bones that have to support all the extra weight.

Rodents and dog food are high-fat foods. They have higher fat contents than the prey of a wild monitor will normally contain. Neither of these items is a good staple to feed your monitor. Monitors routinely fed these items are prone to obesity and all its related health issues. When a monitor is obese, fat gets deposited in the liver, impairing its function. However, before the liver fails, heart failure often occurs.

Obesity and a high-fat diet will also cause high uric acid levels in the bloodstream. This can cause visceral gout, a painful condition in which uric acid crystals form in the abdominal organs. Also, uroliths, solid obstructions composed mainly of uric acid, can occur in the urinary tract. If not removed surgically, they can cause blockage and a painful death for the African monitor lizard (Speers, pers. obs.). Apparently, a high-fat diet has dire consequences for African monitor lizards. Rodents, raw or cooked meat, and dog food are primary sources for visceral gout.

Overfeeding the right foods can also lead to obesity and associated problems. Do not overfeed your monitors. See Chapter 5 for complete feeding instructions.

Finding a Reptile Vet

It is not always easy to find vets who are experienced with reptiles and amphibians. Here are some suggestions to help you locate a vet who can help with your pet monitor. It is best if you locate one before you actually have an emergency.

- **Call veterinarians listed as "exotic" or "reptile" vets in the phonebook. Ask them questions to be sure they are familiar with monitors.**
- **Ask at your local pet stores, herpetological society, animal shelters, and zoos to see if there is someone they can recommend.**
- **Contact the Association of Reptilian and Amphibian Veterinarians. Their website is www.arav.org.**

To avoid obesity in your captive monitor lizard, offer it an enhanced environment where it can exercise and is able to lift its body off the ground through climbing and jumping. Offer a good, varied diet; an occasional small rodent or boiled chicken is alright.

Parasites

In monitor lizards, parasites come in two forms: parasites you can see on the outside of the animal's body (ectoparasites) and parasites inside the animal's body (endoparasites). Parasites drain the body of blood, food, or other resources. Most captive-bred monitors will not have parasites.

Destroy parasites whenever possible. Ticks, pinworms, and other parasites can kill an animal under duress. Being removed from its native lands, shipped for 15 hours or more to a foreign land, placed into a box full of other monitor lizards and reptiles, and then deposited into a cattle trough or terrarium so different from their natural enviornment is very stressful and causes impairment of the immune system. Most of the animals transported in this way succumb to the stress, and the parasites within them contribute to their decline and death, because they are too stressed to fight them off.

Wild-caught monitors frequently have ticks in their nostrils.

Ticks

The most frequently encountered ectoparasites are ticks, relatives of mites and spiders. The monitor tick (*Amblyomma exornatum*) is a blind, eight-legged parasite most often encountered on wild and imported African monitor lizards. Many of these tick species are

Signs of an Unhealthy Monitor

If your monitor displays any of the signs in the list below, it may need veterinary attention. If you are in doubt, it is better to seek the opinion of a veterinarian with experience in reptile medicine than to wait and see what happens. The sooner the animal sees the vet, the greater the chance it will recover.

- **abnormal feces—runny, odd color, excessive odor, worms**
- **inability to right itself when turned upside down**
- **leg not being used or hanging useless**
- **listless or sluggish behavior**
- **refusing food**
- **shedding problems—especially if skin is constricting toes, feet, or limbs**
- **unexplained weight loss**
- **vomiting**

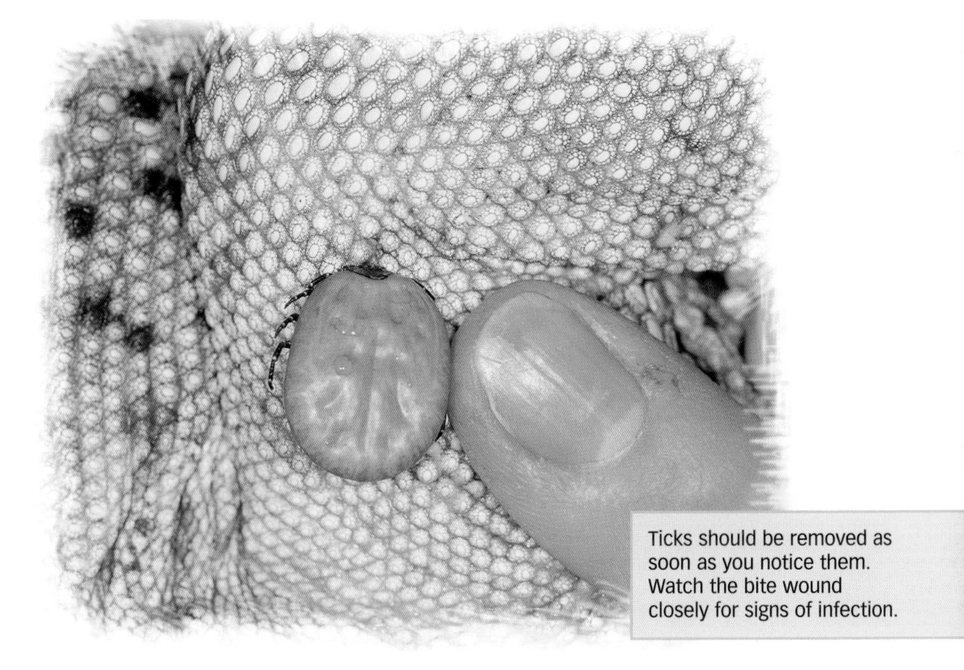

Ticks should be removed as soon as you notice them. Watch the bite wound closely for signs of infection.

exclusive to African monitors. Female ticks are larger than male ticks. Ticks suck blood and can usually be found in the nostrils, armpits, between the toes, and around the tail-base and cloaca areas.

When you get your new monitor lizard, inspect it closely. If you find ticks, remove them using tweezers and gently pulling them out by the head, which is often imbedded into the lizard's skin. Once removed, place the ticks in a jar of rubbing alcohol to kill them.

Healthy monitor lizards are able to remove ticks from their own bodies using an ingenious method. The white-throated monitor lizard has been observed tick grooming itself! If the ticks are between its toes or even in its armpit, the monitor uses its double-keeled tail to scrape the ticks off of its body. It then picks up the tick with its own mouth, crushes it with a power-bite, spits it out, and, using its chin, smashes it like an anvil (Williams and Bayless, 2000). No other monitor lizard species has been observed in tick grooming behavior.

Monitor ticks carry pathogens, such as the bacteria *Coxiella burneti* and *Rickettsia pijperi*, which can cripple a monitor lizard for life. *Coxiella* can cause Q-fever in humans (Wright, 1993; Bayless and Simmons, 2000). Ticks, sand flies, and the nefarious tsetse fly also transmit *Haemogregarines*, or saurian malaria, which can cripple and eventually kill a monitor lizard (Hoogstraal, 1956). Ticks are a vector for heartwater (*Rickettsia ruminanantium*), which is a serious disease of ruminant animals (Burridge, 2000).

Ticks and Abscesses From 1990 to 1993, noted monitor expert Dr. Mike Balsai and I corresponded about the swelling of the toes and feet of several savannah monitor lizards. Since 1993, this malady has been seen in savannah monitors, white-throated monitors, and in tegus (*Tupinambis spp.*) (Balsai, 1993, 1997d). The malady appeared first as a swelling of the toes, sometimes the feet, and even effecting lower leg extremities. Swelling in tissues causes blood vessels to be squeezed, so blood movement below the point of swelling ceases and the tissue can die, becoming gangrenous. The toes often fall off, then if not treated, the feet. I have seen one savannah monitor with three of its feet missing.

Savannah monitors that are kept in overly moist and dirty conditions often develop foot infections. This one was allowed to progress to the point where the bone is now exposed.

One cause of the foot abscesses appears to be the bacterium *Clostridium sordelli*, which can be successfully treated with chloramphenicol (Dull, pers. com.). Monitor keeper R. Williams noted these abscesses in his group of white-throated monitors occurred where ticks were found. He removed the ticks and applied rubbing alcohol to the bitten sites and the swellings quickly diminished (Williams, pers. com.). However, in the case of savannah monitors, the swelling not only persevered, but it left some lizards with amputated feet. These monitors, and later South American tegus, also became afflicted with this malady, which can wane and return on a seasonal basis from November to February (Balsai and Bayless, 1993; Balsai, 1997d). It is suspected to be a reaction of stress, climate changes, and perhaps unsanitary living conditions. With each attack of foot abscess, the condition gets worse, disappears, and can return the following November. It is a perplexing affliction, and one I would like to better understand. I have not heard of another case of foot abscess since 1997. It is not certain that the ticks were the vector for the illness or not, but Williams' observations do support this idea.

Worms: Cestodes and Nematodes

Various species of worm can infest monitors. Usually, they infest the digestive tract, but there are some that inhabit the lungs, bloodstream, liver, and subcutaneous tissues. Among parasitic worms, the cestode (flatworm) *Tanqua tiara* is the most often encountered parasite. It is a bone-white colored pinworm sometimes seen in the mouth and feces of newly imported wild African monitor lizards. It can be effectively treated with fenbendazole. See a veterinarian for treatment and dosage amounts.

A particularly nefarious nematode worm is *Angiostrongylus cantonensis*, which apparently gets into the meninges of the brain and spinal cord causing meningoencaphalitis, or "star-gazing" condition. The animal becomes neurologically impaired and is unable to walk or feed. I have seen this affliction in the savannah, white-throated, and water monitor lizards (*Varanus salvator*), and it has always been fatal.

Spic and Span

Most infectious diseases in monitor lizards stem from filthy living conditions. Unsanitary housing leads to increased stress levels, suppressed immune systems, and increased pathogen numbers. Maintain a clean enclosure by removing all droppings as soon as possible, keeping a supply of clean water at your lizard's disposal at all times, and conducting regular and thorough cleanings of the entire enclosure. Warm, clean, and dry living conditions are a hobbyist's first line of defense against diseases in their savannah monitor lizards.

Cryptosporidiosis

Cryptosporidium parvum is a coccidian protozoan that can be passed to humans (Boyer, 1997). By the mid-1990s, cryptosporidiosis was a key concern among herpetoculturalists and epidemiologists. Although most cases of cryptosporidiosis are acquired by humans, reptiles acquire it too (Tucker, pers. com.; Boyer, 1997). Diarrhea is the key symptom of this infection and usually lasts from three to ten days. By ten days, the host may be severely or irreversibly dehydrated and could succumb. A clinical fecal examination by a veterinarian is required to properly identify this organism in your lizard's stool. Until recently, cryptosporidiosis was difficult to treat. In 2000, Dr. T. K. Graczyk of Johns Hopkins University, Baltimore discovered that hyperimmune bovine colostrums (HBC) adequately treats *Cryptosporidium parvum* in savannah monitor lizards. Because of the real risk of contracting this disease from an infected reptile, you must exercise the utmost caution when handling an infected animal or its cage contents.

Heat It Up

When a reptile has an infection, raising cage temperatures slightly can help them ward it off. If your monitor comes down with an infection, raise the cage temperature by 5 degrees or so.

Bacterial Infections

Pseudomonas and *Salmonella* are commonly encountered bacteria in most vertebrates. *Salmonella* is a natural inhabitant of many animals' intestinal tracts, most often found in ruminant and rodent mammal hosts (Mader, 1993). When an animal's immune system is suppressed, bacteria take advantage of this situation and begin to reproduce rapidly. If the salmonella is not stopped with antibiotics, it can invade every organ of the body.

Baby chicks are the most frequent sources of salmonella and can and are readily used as a food source for monitor lizards. This bacterium is not a threat to healthy animals or people. Infection with *Salmonella* is called salmonellosis, although most people just call it salmonella.

Bacterial and protozoan infections can lead to neurological afflictions if they are allowed to progress. Maladies like uncontrollable head tremors and the inability to properly walk are caused by infections of the spinal cord and the brain. These are the same kind of symptoms produced by the nematode *Angiostrongylus cantonensis*, so when your animals have known infections of these kinds, seek veterinary treatment immediately.

In 1992, I received 20 imported white-throated monitor lizards that had systemic salmonellosis, and all but three died. The symptoms included eating zestfully at first, appearing to be their characteristically gluttonous selves. Then they became bloated, suddenly went off feed, and died within two weeks of not eating. It was horrible to watch. Those were rough days for me as I watched these beautiful Tanzanian animals drop off one by one. So when you get a new wild-caught monitor, make sure your veterinarian gives it a thorough examination, inside and out, before bringing it home. If you have other reptiles of any kind, place this new animal in quarantine for at least 30 days (see Chapter 4). In this way, the nasty pathogens can be detected and killed before it is placed into your own collection, where it could contaminate others.

This is why it is important to wash your hands thoroughly before and after interacting with your monitor. It is also highly recommended before and after you enter each terrarium so that you avoid receiving or giving bacterium to other reptiles or yourself. Common sense can save you a lot of grief, hardship, and veterinary and medical bills if you follow these practices consistently.

Mouth Rot

Mouth rot, also known as stomatitis, is a bacterial infection seen in the gums and mouth cavities of reptiles. It appears as a cheesy looking material, which is reptilian pus. Most reptiles with this malady have undergone high stress levels (usually through importation), have been living in filth and squalor, and/or are malnourished. The bacteria that usually cause mouth rot are *Mycobacterium chelonei* and *Pseudomonas aureus*. *Pseudomonas* bacteria prefer wet environments, like the mouths of reptiles, where they can grow and replicate themselves, eventually causing ulcerative inflammation of the mouth cavity. The oral mucous membranes swell so much, the victim cannot close its mouth. The infection will eventually spread into the jaw bone, causing bone loss and jaw degeneration. By this time, the infected animal is completely unable to feed. If left untreated, the animal will die. If you suspect your pet has mouth rot, seek veterinary attention as soon as possible. Successful treatment for mouth rot involves the vet cleaning out the area of the infection and administering antibiotics.

Thermal Burns

Thermal burns are created when the skin of a living thing receives too much thermal radiation. In the case of reptiles, this

If your monitor becomes ill, raising the cage temperatures slightly may help it fight off infection.

Preventing Salmonellosis

Although monitors and most other reptiles carry salmonella bacteria, there are a number of simple things you can do to prevent yourself and your family from becoming infected. Here is a list:

- **always supervise carefully any interaction between children and monitors**
- **disinfect any bathtub or sink used to bathe the monitor**
- **do not eat or drink while handling the monitor or cleaning its cage**
- **keep the monitor and its enclosure clean**
- **never allow your monitor to roam in the kitchen**
- **never kiss your monitor—no matter how cute it is**
- **teach your children proper monitor handling and hygiene**
- **wash you hands after handling your monitor, its waste products, or any items from the enclosure**

usually occurs because of faulty or poorly monitored heating devices. Too much heat exposure at close proximity to your animal will result in burns to your animal's skin. The best way to treat thermal burns is to prevent them in the first place. Monitor the temperatures in your lizard's cage carefully, and use a thermostat on all heating devices to prevent them from overheating. Make sure your monitor cannot come in contact with any light bulbs or other heating equipment.

If your monitor should receive a burn, remove the animal as soon as possible from the enclosure and apply silver sulfadiazine cream (e.g., Silvadine) generously to the burned area. This will reduce the extent of the injury and promote skin healing. Watch the area for infection closely, as burns are prone to infection. If the burn area is small and not deep, the scars of the burn area may disappear within a few sheddings. However, if the burned area is large, bleeding, or blackened, then veterinary care is required. Severe burns can cause serious dehydration, so seek veterinary care as soon as possible. You will also have to adjust your cage heating methods so that future burns do not occur.

Concluding Remarks

I think we have answered to Dr. Harry Hoogstraal's commentary regarding the African savannah monitor, "One cannot understand an organism until one understands how it relates to others." We have seen that even with the associated pressures of life in Africa—establishing a home range by finding adequate temperature ranges, safe hide spots, adequate food and water, avoiding predators and parasites, and mating proclivities—these animals are very adaptable and intelligent, which makes them highly desirable to keepers.

Monitor lizards are marvelous, intelligent, dinosaur-like reptiles. There is a delicate balance between the reptile and its habits, nutrition, and disease. As long as this balance is maintained, life and longevity ensues. Hopefully, with the information presented here, you and your reptilian roommate will have a happy and healthy experience together. The care and well-being of a monitor lizard is as important as that of any pet—if you cannot commit to that care, go buy a sock monkey. I hope your cohabitation with these marvelous animals will be a rewarding and most enjoyable experience for you.

For your theatrical enjoyment, the only African "savannah" monitor depicted in Hollywood films is the white-throated monitor (*Varanus albigularis*), which appeared in the following films:

- *Animals are Beautiful People* (1974). Produced by Jamie Uys. 92 min.
- *Castles of Clay* (1978). Survival Television, Anglia Television Ltd., England. 60 min., documentary.
- *Gods Must be Crazy, The* (1986). 109 min.
- *Kingdom of the Snake* (1998). NDR Naturfilm, Wildfilm cc, Hamburg. 50 min., documentary.
- *Mysterious Spring - Africa's Mzima* (1972). Anglia Television, Ltd. England. Produced by A. and J. Root. 60 min., documentary.
- *Naked Prey, The* (1966). 96 min.
- *Tusks* (1990). 99 min.

Acknowledgment

I sincerely thank Tom Mazorlig for allowing me to publish this work in this venue. I thank Debbie Carton, Bernd Eidenmuller, Betty Gordon, Paul Gritis, Dr. Hans-Georg Horn, Pete Strimple, and Karl H. Switak for help with translations during the research phase of this book.

I also thank Dr. Kraig Adler, John Adragna, Kevin Baker, Dr. Mike Balsai, Dr. Gordon Bell, Daniel Bennett, Dr. Sean Blamires, Dr. William R. Branch (PEM), Dr. Donald G. Broadley, Dr. Vivian de Buffrenil, Dr. Jim Bull, Dr. Michael J. Burridge, Dr. John Cloudsley-Thompson (Emeritus), Michael Corwin, Jerry Cowan, Dr. David Crews, Kalthleen Davidson (Hogle Zoo), Ann Day, Dr. Carlos Drewes, Andrew F. Dull, DVM, Dave Durham, Quetzal Dwyer, East Bay Vivarium (EBV), E. J. Edwards, Juan J. Edwards, Clay Fischer, Steve Ford, Greg Greer, Mike Griffin, Robert Guzewicz, Gerald V. Haagner, Shawn Henderson, Robert Holveck, Dr. Hans-Georg Horn, Dr. Adel A. Ibrahim "Iggy" Ihren, Dr. Ivan Ineich (MNHN), Brian Keshner, Dr. Dave Kirschner, Dr, Michael Lambert, Bob Larson (Hogle Zoo), Juan M. Laulhe, Dr. Raymond F. Laurent, Jeff Lemm, (late) Ben Loots, Rob MacInnes, Gregg Madden, Robyn Markland (ProExotics), Dr. Colin McCarthy (BMNH), Jim McDavid, Duane Meier (Honolulu Zoo), (late) Dr. Sherman Minton, D. R. Morgan, Scott Moser, Greg Naclerio, David Nieves, Wanda Olson, Bivash Pandav, Siegfried Reinshagen, Steven Rippy, Paul Rodriguez, Andy Rowell, Ron and Stella St. Pierre, Scott Schumm, Dr. Karl P. Shuker, Leigh-Anne Simmons, Jerry Sloan, Stephen Spawls, Becky Speer, Dr. Michael Stanner, Colby Strebe, Pete Strimple, Dr. Sam Sweet, Karl H. Switak, Jeff Terptipes, Andrew G. Thompson, Suzanne Tucker, Gerard Visser, Gurbe v.d. Wal, Bryan Waterloo, Ronnie Watt, Rodney Williams, Dr. Jan Wolters, and Pete Zupich for their generosity, friendship, and for sharing information—and after all, sharing is what science is all about!

Alberts, A. 1994. Off to see the Lizard: Lessons from the wild. *Vivarium*, March/April, 5(5):26-28.

Attum, O., R.L. Earley, M. Bayless, and P. Easoni. 2000. The Agnostic Behaviour of Bosc's Monitor (*Varanus exanthematicus* Bosc, 1792) in captivity. *Herpetological Bulletin* 73:22-26.

Auerbach, R.D. 1987. The Amphibians and Reptiles of Botswana. Mokwepa Consultants, Gaborone. 295p.

Balsai, M. 1992. *The General Care and Maintenance of Savannah Monitors and Other Popular Monitor Species.* Advanced Vivarium Systems, Lakeside. 55p.

Balsai, M. 1997a. Controversies about rodent diets for Savannah Monitors. *Vivarium*, May/June, 8(5):18-19.

Balsai, M. 1997b. Monitors and Omnivory. *Vivarium*, July/August, 8(6):73.

Balsai, M. 1997c. Diets for Monitors. *Vivarium*, Dec./Jan., 9(1):13,

Balsai, M. 1997d. Bizarre Subcutaneous Abscesses in Tegus Too? *Vivarium*, Dec./Jan., 9(1):24.

Balsai, M. and M.K. Bayless. 1993. Bizarre subcutaneous abscesses and possible causes in the savannah monitor lizard, *Varanus exanthematicus*. *VaraNews* 3(3):7-10.

Barbour, T. 1926. *Reptiles and Amphibians*. Houghton Mifflin and Company, Cambridge. 125p.

Bartlett, R.D. and P. Bartlett. 1997. *Lizard Care from A to Z*. Barrons Educational Series, Inc., Hauppauge. 178p.

Bayless, M.K. 1994. Zur Fortpflanzungsbiologie des Steppenwarans (*Varanus exanthematicus*). *Salamandra* 30(2):109-118.

Bayless, M.K. 1997. The distribution of African monitor lizards (Sauria: Varanidae). *African Journal of Ecology* 35:374-377.

Bayless, M.K. 2002. Monitor Lizards: a pan-African check-list of their Zoogeography (Sauria: Varanidae: Polydaedalus). *Journal of Biogeography* 29:1643-1701.

Bayless, M.K. and L. Luiselli. 2000. A review of the Predation upon African monitor Lizards (Varanidae). *Bulletin Societe Herpetologie Francais* 95:67-74.

Bayless, M.K., G.C. Akani, and L. Luiselli. 2003. Daudin's Monitor (*Varanus ornatus*, Daudin, 1803) and its association with Ubani (Bonny Island), Southern Nigeria. *Herpetological Bulletin* 83:2-6.

Bayless, M.K. and R. Huffaker. 1992. Observations of Egg Deposition and Hatching of the Savannah Monitor (*Varanus exanthematicus* Bosc 1792) in Captivity. *VaraNews*

3(1):5-6.

Bayless, M.K. and B. Pierson. 2003. *Varanus niloticus* (Nile monitor): captive adult feeding on ants. *Herpetological Bulletin* 85:29-30.

Bayless, M.K. and T. Reynolds. 1992. Breeding of the Savannah Monitor Lizard in Captivity (*Varanus exanthematicus* Bosc, 1792). *Herpetology (S.W. Herpetologists Society)* 22(1):12-14.

Bayless, M.K. and L.A. Simmons. 2000. Tick parasites on the rock monitor lizard (*Varanus albigularis* Daudin, 1802) of Tanzania, Africa. *African Journal of Ecology* 38:363-364.

Bayless, M.K. and R.G. Sprackland. 2000a. The Taxonomy of Africa's Savannah & Cape Monitor Lizards. *Reptiles Magazine*, June, 8(6):76-85.

Bayless, M.K. and R.G. Sprackland. 2000b. The Taxonomy of Africa's Savannah & Cape Monitor Lizards, Part II. *Reptiles Magazine*, July, 8(7):40-47.

Bennett, D. 1992. Bosc monitor lizard. *Reptilian magazine* 1(2):25-27.

Bennett, D. 1998. *Monitor Lizards*. Chimaira Editions, Frankfurt. 352p.

Bennett, D. 2000. Preliminary data on the diet of juvenile *Varanus exanthematicus* (Sauria: Varanidae) in the coastal plain of Ghana. *Herpetological Journal* 10:75-76.

Bennett, D. and R. Thakoordyal. 2003. *The Savannah Monitor Lizard. The Truth About Varanus exanthematicus*. Viper Press, Glossop. 83p.

Berry, H. and G. Cubitt. 1989. *Etosha National Park*. Struil Publishers, Cape Town. 24p.

Blamires, S.J. 2001. Influence of Temperature on Burrow Use by the Monitor Lizard *Varanus panoptes* of the Coastal Dunes at Fog Bay, Northern Australia. *Asiatic Herpetological Research* 9:25-29.

Bohme, W. 1997. Robert Mertens' Systematik und Klassifikation der Warane: Aktualisierung seiner 1942er Monographie und eine revidierte Checkliste. pIII-XXIII. IN: Reprint *Die Familie der Warane (Varanidae)* By Robert F. Mertens (1942a-c). Senckenberg Museum, Frankfurt. 391p.

Borland, D.L. 1968. Monitor Lizard. *The Lammergeyer* 8:54.

Boyer, T.H. 1997. Comments on Husbandry and Medical Problems in Captive Varanids. *Varanids* 1(1):4-11.

Brana, F. 1996. Sexual dimorphism in lacertid lizards: male head increase vs. female abdomen increase? *Oikos* 75:511-523.

Branch, W.R. 1988. *Varanus exanthematicus albigularis* Rock Leguaan Egg Size. *Journal of the Herpetological Association of Africa* 35:39.

Branch, W.R. 1991. The Regenia Registers of "Gogga" Brown (1869-1909) "Memoranda on a species of Monitor or Varan." *Mertensiella* 2:57-110.

Buffenstein, R. and G. Louw. 1982. Temperature effects on bioenergetics of growth, assimilation efficiency and thyroid activity in juvenile varanid lizards. *Journal of Thermal Biology* 7:197-200.

Buffrenil, V.d. and H. Francillon-Viellot. 2001. Ontogenetic changes in bone compactness in male and female Nile monitors (*Varanus niloticus*). *Journal of Zoology London* 254:539-546.

Burridge, M.J. 2001. Ticks (Acari: Ixodidae) spread by the international trade in reptiles and their potential roles in dissemination of diseases. *Bulletin of Entomological Research* 91:3-23.

Burridge, M.J., L.-A. Simmons, and S.A. Allan. 2000. Introduction of potential Heartwater vectors and other exotic ticks into Florida on imported reptiles. *Journal of Parasitology* 86(4):700-704.

Christian, A., H.-G. Horn, et.al. 1994. Bipedie bei rezenten Reptilien. *Natur und Museum* 124(2):45-57.

Cisse, M. 1972. L'alimentation des Varanides au Senegal (The Diet of Varanids in Senegal). *Bulletin de L'Institut Fondamental Afrique Noire* 34A(2):503-515.

Cisse, M. 1976. Le cycle genital des Varans du Senegal (Reptiles Lacertilians). *Bulletin de l'Institut Fondamental Afrique Noire* 38A(1):188-205.

Cloudsley-Thompson, J.L. 1999. *The Diversity of Amphibians and Reptiles*. An Introduction. Springer-Verlag, Berlin. 254p.

Coborn, J. 1994. *Savannah Monitors*. T.F.H. Publications, Neptune City. 64p.

Dieter, C. 1997. Keeping and Breeding the Black-throated Monitor. *Reptile Hobbyist*, October, 3(2):10-15.

Duinen, J.J.v. 1983. Varanenkweek in het Noorderierenpark te Emmen. *Lacerta*, Oktober, 42(1):12-14.

Erickson, G.M., A.d. Ricqles, V.d. Buffrenil, R.E. Molnar, and M.K. Bayless. 2003. Vermiform bones and the Evolution of Gigantism in *Megalania*—how a reptilian fox became a lion. *Journal of Vertebrate Paleontology* 23(4):966-970.

Falk, K. 1921. Sudwestarikanische reptilien und ihre Heimat. *Wochenschriften Aquarien Terrarium*

18(14):231-232.

Faust, R.J. 2001. *Nile Monitors*. Barron's Educational Series, Hauppauge. 95p.

Firth, I. 2003. Response of monitor lizards to a food source; Evidence for association learning? *Herpetological Bulletin* 84:1-4.

Grenot, C. 1968. Etude comparative de la resistance a la chaleur d'*Uromastyx acanthinurus* et de *Varanus griseus*. *Terre Vie* 22:390-409.

Hediger, H. 1964. *Wild Animals in Captivity*. Dover Publications, Inc. New York. 207p.

Heidger, H. 1968. *The Psychology and Behaviour of Animals in Zoos and Circuses*. Dover Publications, Inc., New York. 166p.

Hoogstraal, H. 1956. *African Ixodoidea*. Ticks of the Sudan. Volume I. Department of the Navy Bureau of Medicine and Surgery. 1101p [sadly, Volume II was never published].

Horn, H.-G., M. Gaulke, and W. Bohme. 1994. New data on ritualized combats in monitor lizards (Sauria: Varanidae), with remarks on their function and phylogenetic implications. *Zoological Garden* 64(5):265-280.

Horn, H.-G. and G.J. Visser. 1997. Review of reproduction of Monitor lizards (*Varanus sp.*) in captivity II. *International Zoo Yearbook* 35:227-246.

Ibrahim, A.A. 2000. A radiotelemetric study of the body temperature of *Varanus griseus* (Sauria: Varanidae) in Zaranik Protected Area, North Sinai, Egypt. *Egyptian Journal of Biology* 2:57-66.

Irvine, F.R. 1960. Lizards and crocodiles as food for Man. *British Journal of Herpetology* 2:197-202.

Irwin, S., B. Lyons, and T. Frisby. 1996. Nocturnal activity by *Varanus panoptes* at Cape Melville. *Herpetofauna* 26(2):50.

Jeungst, M. 1997. Landscaping for Lizards. *ZooNooz*, April, 70(4):28-30.

Karmanova, I.C. 1975. New data on the circadian rythms of waking and sleeping in vertebrates. *Doklady Biological Sciences* 225(6):576-578.

Krebs, U. 1991. Ethology and Learning: from observation to semi-natural experiment. *Mertensiella* 2:220-232.

LaBenda, W. 2001. Enriching the lives of your captive herps. *Reptile & Amphibian Hobbyist*, July, 6(11):40-42.

Lemm, J. 1996. Monitors on the Mesa. *ZooNooz*, June, 69(6):10-14.

Lemm, J. 1997. Diets for Monitors. *Vivarium*, Dec./Jan., 9(1):13.

Lemm, J.M. 1998. White-Throated Monitor (*Varanus albigularis*). *Reptiles*, February, 6(2):10-12,

14-16, 18, 20-21.

Lenz, S. 1995. Zur Biologie und Okologie des Nilwarans, *Varanus niloticus* (Linnaeus 1766) in Gambia, Westafrika. *Mertensiella* 5:1-256.

Mertens, R.F. 1926.Zur Kenntis der Herpetofauna vom Angola. *Senckenbergiana* 8(3/4):150-154.

Mertens, R.F. 1942a-c. Der Familie der Warane (Varanidae). *Abhandlungen der Senckenbergischen Naturforschenden Gesellschaft* (a)462:1-116; (b)465:117-234; (c)466:235-391.

Miles, M.A., A.G. Thompson and G.W. Walters. 1978. *Bulletin de l'Institut Fondamental Afrique Noire* 40A(2):437-456.

Miller, M. 1966. The Cochlear duct of Lizards. *Proceedings of the California Academy of Sciences*, Series 4, 33(11):255-359.

Muller, L. 1905a-b. Der Westafrikanische Steppenwaran (*Varanus exanthematicus* Bosc). *Blatter Aquarien Terrarien Kunde* (a)16(27):266-268; (b)16(28):274-276.

Owen, R. 1840-1845. *Odontography*. Volume I-II. Hippolyte Bailliere, Publishers, London. (I) 655p.

Philip, K.M. 1999. Niche Partitioning of *Varanus doreanus*, *V. indicus* and *V. jobiensis* in Irian Jaya: Preliminary results. *Mertensiella* 11:307-316.

Pianka, E.R., D. King and R. King. 2004. *Varanoid Lizards of the World*. Indiana University Press, Bloomington. 588p.

Schmidt, K.P. 1919 (1998). Contributions to the Herpetology of the American Congo Expedition, 1909-1915. *Bulletin of the American Museum of Natural History* 39:385-62 (Reprinted by the S.S.A.R., 1998, 780p.).

Schmidt, R.S. 1964. Phylogenetic Significance of Lizard Cochlea. *Copeia* 3:542-549.

Sinclair,A.G. and R.M. Alexander. 1987. Estimates of forces exerted by the jaw muscles of some Reptiles. *Journal of Zoology London* 213:107-115.

Smythe, R.H. 1975. *Vision in the Animal World*. St. Martin's Press, New York. 165p.

Soule, M. 1972. On the Climatic determination of scale size in a lizard. *Systematic Zoology* 21(1):97-105.

Visser, G.J. 1981. Breeding the White-throated monitor (*Varanus exanthematicus albigularis*) at Rotterdam Zoo. *International Zoo Yearbook* 21:87-91.

Warburg, M.R. 1965. Studies on the Environmental Physiology of some Australian Lizards from arid and semi-arid habitats. *Australian Journal of Zoology* 13:563-575.

Watt, R. 1999. *Veld-Focus.* Ten Years of Nature's Wonders. Rapid Commercial Print Brokers, The Reeds, RSA. 150p.

Werner, F. 1907. XII. Die Reptilien und Amphibien. *Sitzungsberichte der Academie der Wissenschaften* 116(I):1823-1926 + PL I-II.

Wesiak, K. 1998. Uber ein bemerkenswertes Paarungsverhalten vom Sudafrikanischen Kapwaran *Varanus albigularis* (Daudin, 1802) im terrarium. Monitor (DGHT) 7(1):23-29.

Williams, R. and M.K. Bayless. 1998. Tick removal behavior by a White-throat Monitor lizard (*Varanus albigularis*) (Sauria: Varanidae). *Bulletin of the Chicago Herpetological Society* 33(5):101-102.

Witte, G.d. 1953. Reptiles. *Exploration du Parc National de l'Upemba* 6:1-322.

Wolters, J. 1990. *On the anatomy of descending pathways from the brain stem to the spinal cord in a lizard Varanus exanthematicus.* CIP-Data Koninklijke Bibliotheek, Den Haag. 185p.

Wright, K. 1993. Suggested Quarantine procedures for Monitors and Tegus. *Vivarium,* Nov./Dec., 5(3):22-23.

Yeboah, S. 1993. Aspects of the biology of two sympatric species of monitor lizards *Varanus niloticus* and *Varanus exanthematicus* (Reptilia, Sauria) in Ghana. *African Journal of Ecology* 32:331-333.

Young, B.A. 1997. On the absence of Taste Buds in Monitor Lizards (*Varanus*) and Snakes. *Journal of Herpetology* 31(1):130-137.

Young, Bruce et.al. 1998. Acoustic analysis of the defensive sounds of *Varanus salvator* with notes on sound production on other varanid species. *Hamadryad* 23(1):1-14.

Young, E. 1965. *Amblyomma exornatum* (Koch) as a cause of mortality among monitors. *Journal of the South African Veterinarians Medical Association* 36(4):579.

CLUBS AND SOCIETIES

Amphibian, Reptile & Insect Association
Liz Price
23 Windmill Rd
Irthlingsborough
Wellingborough NN9 5RJ
England

American Society of Ichthyologists and Herpetologists
Maureen Donnelly, Secretary
Grice Marine Laboratory
Florida International University
Biological Sciences
11200 SW 8th St.
Miami, FL 33199
Telephone: (305) 348-1235
E-mail: asih@fiu.edu
www.asih.org

Society for the Study of Amphibians and Reptiles (SSAR)
Marion Preest, Secretary
The Claremont Colleges
925 N. Mills Ave.
Claremont, CA 91711
Telephone: 909-607-8014
E-mail: mpreest@jsd.claremont.edu
www.ssarherps.org

VETERINARY RESOURCES

Association of Reptile and Amphibian Veterinarians (ARAV)
P.O. Box 605
Chester Heights, PA 19017
Phone: 610-358-9530
Fax: 610-892-4813
E-mail: ARAVETS@aol.com
www.arav.org

RESCUE AND ADOPTION SERVICES

ASPCA
424 East 92nd Street
New York, NY 10128-6801
Phone: (212) 876-7700
E-mail: information@aspca.org
www.aspca.org

New England Amphibian and Reptile Rescue
www.nearr.com

Petfinder.com
www.petfinder.org

Reptile Rescue, Canada
http://www.reptilerescue.on.ca

RSPCA (UK)
Wilberforce Way
Southwater
Horsham, West Sussex RH13 9RS
Telephone: 0870 3335 999
www.rspca.org.uk

WEBSITES

CITES (Convention on International Trade in Endangered Species of Wild Fauna and Flora)
www.cites.org

Federation of British Herpetologists
www.F-B-H.co.uk

Herp Station
http://www.petstation.com/herps.html

Kingsnake.com
http://www.kingsnake.com

Melissa Kaplan's Herp Care Collection
http://www.anapsid.org/boa.html

Reptile Forums
http://reptileforums.com/forums/

Reptile Rooms, The
http://www.reptilerooms.org

Savannah Monitor Diet
http://www.anapsid.org/balsai.html

Varanid Information Network
http://www.varanus.net/

Varanus.co.uk
http://www.varanus.co.uk/

Varanus.nl (in Dutch and English)
http://www.varanus.nl/

MAGAZINES

Herp Digest
www.herpdigest.org

Reptiles Magazine
P.O. Box 6050
Mission Viejo, CA 92690
www.animalnetwork.com/reptiles

Reptilia Magazine
Salvador Mundi 2
Spain-08017 Barcelona
Subscripciones-subscriptions@reptilia.org

Boldface numbers indicate illustrations; t indicates a table.

Photo Credits:

Kevin. Baker: 101
Joan Balzarini: 38, 102
R. D. Bartlett: 22, 42, 57, 88
Allen Both: 8, 31, 40
Marius Burger: 37
Chris Dieter: 97, 99
Sean McKeown: 24
Isabelle Francais: 6, 30, 46, 66, 67, 76, and front cover
Paul Freed: 14, 34, 35, 73, 82, 86, 100, 107, 108
Erik Loza: 90
W. P. Mara: 19 (bottom)
G. & C. Merker: 75, 87
Robert Pearcy: 70
Carol Polich: 55, 72
Michael Smoker: 79, 81
K. H. Switak: 1, 4, 12, 19 (top), 106

All other photos are courtesy of Mark K. Bayless.